THE
DUCK
COMMANDER

DEVOTIONAL
for Couples

AL AND LISA ROBERTSON

HOWARD BOOKS
AN IMPRINT OF SIMON & SCHUSTER, INC.

New York   Nashville   London   Toronto   Sydney   New Delhi

Howard Books
An Imprint of Simon & Schuster, Inc.
1230 Avenue of the Americas
New York, NY 10020

First Howard Books hardcover edition February 2016

HOWARD and colophon are trademarks of Simon & Schuster, Inc.

For information about special discounts for bulk purchases, please contact Simon & Schuster Special Sales at 1-866-506-1949 or business@simonandschuster.com.

The Simon & Schuster Speakers Bureau can bring authors to your live event. For more information or to book an event, contact the Simon & Schuster Speakers Bureau at 1-866-248-3049 or visit our website at www.simonspeakers.com.

Interior design by Akasha Archer

Manufactured in the United States of America

10   9   8   7   6   5   4   3   2   1

Library of Congress Cataloging-in-Publication Data

Names: Robertson, Alan, 1965–
Title: The Duck commander devotional for couples / Al and Lisa Robertson.
Description: Nashville, TN : Howard Books, 2016.
Identifiers: LCCN 2015036985
Subjects: LCSH: Married people—Prayers and devotions.
Classification: LCC BV4596.M3 R637 2016 | DDC 242/.644—dc23 LC record available at http://lccn.loc.gov/2015036985

ISBN 978-1-5011-2620-8
ISBN 978-1-5011-2621-5 (ebook)

Contents

INTRODUCTION

ONE OF THE greatest blessings of being married for many years is that at some point you're able to look back and appreciate things you were too busy to recognize when they were actually happening. We look back now and realize that every ounce of energy and every moment of time that we invested in growing our relationship was absolutely worth it! The book is our attempt to add a great blessing to *your* marriage. The topics you will read about here come from our experiences and the experiences of those we have worked with for the past fifteen years. *Honesty* and *forgiveness* are repeated topics throughout this book, as they have proven to be the most vital virtues in our relationship for maintaining marital health and dynamic love.

We considered whether to use a daily or weekly format as we compiled this book. We firmly believe in the value of daily devotion time with God, but our experience has been that it is very difficult for couples to come together every day of the week because of the many demands on their time. So we have designed this book to help you spend time together at least once a week to strengthen your relationship with God and with each other.

We ourselves have struggled with starting and maintaining devotional time together, so we encourage you not give up on this important endeavor. If you miss a week or so, just pick up where you left off and keep going. If you find you have more time to dedicate to this journey, then by all means meet together more than once a week. We know how important it is to spend regular time together sharing in God's word and sharing your hearts in discussion and prayer. We encourage you to dedicate at least thirty to forty-five minutes a week to this book and to each other.

When we invest time and energy into our relationship, that time always brings blessings and growth that allow us to keep building on the future.

Each week in this devotional begins with a story or devotional thought and a scripture from the Bible. We will call this section God's Blueprint, because we know how important it is that your relationship be designed around God's plan for marriage. Then, in the Home Improvement section, we've provided a few simple questions to help you explore your relationship and yourselves. You'll also find a few blank lines in this section where you can record your thoughts on what you've talked about together. You may prefer to write out your thoughts in personal journals—either way, the writing helps you put your thoughts into words and provides a record to look back on so that you can see the progress you've made.

Each devotional will close with a section we call Team Building. This is time spent in prayer with your partner, asking God to help guide your relationship. It is one of the most important parts of your time together, and we guarantee it will help you grow closer to God and to each other. We have included our own prayers as examples of how we asked God to help us in certain stages of our relationship—

with Him and with each other. We encourage you to pray in your own words, out loud and together. We'll remind you to do this every week, because it's not always comfortable. So if you haven't done this before, it may seem difficult and awkward at first. But trust us, it will get easier and your relationship will grow in unbelievable ways if you keep at it.

If all this is new for you, then we encourage you to take your time and give it a chance. Topics we feel are easier to address will be covered in the beginning of the book and we'll then transition into more challenging topics as you progress and become more comfortable with the process.

If this material is not new to you, and you are used to spending devotional time together and want to plow through this book in a few weeks rather than a year, then we salute you and hope it helps you grow closer to each other. Either way, your investment of time, energy, and resources in doing this devotional will make you stronger and will help you grow closer to each other. Already we have been blessed by our time spent putting this book together and bringing the blessings of God's Word into our relationship.

We've written this book largely with married couples in mind, but it's also a great study for seriously dating or engaged couples.

We pray for your relationship and your family and would love to hear how this book has helped you grow closer to each other. If you'd like to share anything with us, please send us a note at duckcommanderdevoforcouples@gmail.com and let us know how you are doing. God bless you as you start this incredible journey to grow closer.

—*Al & Lisa Robertson*

<u>WEEK 1</u>

THE STORY OF US

LISA: We love hearing stories of how couples met, fell in love, and wound up getting married. There is a unique quality to every couple and how their relationship unfolded. Our own story is a testament of how crazy love can be! I loved Al from the moment I laid my eyes on him in our little country middle school way back in 1977. I was a gawky sixth grader, and he was a brand-new eighth grader all the girls were after. I can't explain why, but somehow I knew that one day we would be together and he would be my knight in shining armor!

AL: I never even noticed my younger admirer because I was too busy enjoying all the attention I was getting from other girls! Not until the last days of my senior year in high school did Lisa finally catch my eye, but unfortunately, my life was spiraling out of control with drugs and alcohol. Also unfortunately, I took advantage of Lisa's love and treated her badly, then broke her heart on my way out of town. After coming to my senses and coming home to Christ and my family, I remembered that girl who loved me so deeply, and I reached out to see if she might be willing to reconnect.

LISA: I went into my own tailspin when Alan left me, and I had a lot of bad experiences with guys. When he called me after two years,

I should have been furious, but instead I was elated. This was the man I had always known I would spend the rest of my life with. We started dating again, and within a year we were married and building a family and life together.

For the past thirty years we have had our share of ups and downs, but we are still in love and growing in our relationship every day. We give glory to God for delivering us from past mistakes and live daily to meet the needs of each other. We pray for a future that deepens our family legacy of faith and ultimately leads to everlasting life in heaven.

We encourage you to appreciate the uniqueness of your mate and be willing to give each other the best of what God has given you.

God's Blueprint: *Putting God's Word into Your Relationship*

Read the following scripture together and out loud.

PSALM 107:1–2

GIVE THANKS TO THE LORD, FOR HE IS GOOD;
HIS LOVE ENDURES FOREVER. LET THE REDEEMED
OF THE LORD TELL THEIR STORY.

Think back to when you first met and share your unique stories with each other.

1. When did you know that you wanted to spend the rest of your life with each other?
2. What obstacles did you have to overcome in order to be together? Think about your individual and "together" issues.
3. What positive action did your loved one take to help overcome these obstacles?
4. Looking back, did those obstacles help and/or hurt your relationship? In what ways?
5. Do you believe God played a part in your being together? If so, how?

Home Improvement: *Start Where You Are and Grow*

1. What goals did you have when you first got married?
2. Have you met those goals? If so, how? If not, then why not?
3. What goals do you hope to reach in the future?
4. Share personal goals as well as goals for your relationship together.

Record some of the goals you hope to reach in the future. Then you can refer to your notes later to see how you have grown.

HER THOUGHTS

1. graduate 2. controlling my temper when walter pushes my buttons 3. not to yell @ Walt or future kids 4. stay together.

1. start taking steps toward kids 2. figure out career in Marine Corps ☻ 3. More involved @ church 4. Care more about others

Team Building: *Grow Closer to Each Other as You Talk to God Together*

You may not be used to praying together, but give it a try—even if you're nervous. When your hearts are open to God in prayer, you'll find that many of your defenses toward each other melt away. Read our prayers together—maybe the men can read Al's and the women read Lisa's—and then pray your own prayers out loud.

AL: Lord, I am very grateful you watched over us as we got our acts together and found one another. Thank you for your grace, which offered me new hope and allowed me to see my bride for the woman you made her to be. We are grateful for the years and for the uniqueness of us. We look forward to being with you in heaven, forever, because of Christ, amen.

LISA: Father, I am so thankful you blessed me with my soul mate. It took a while and at times looked doubtful, but you knew just when the timing was right. Thank you, God, for your perfect timing. Thirty-plus years ago I said "I do" and I still say I do. Please, Father, be with us for the next thirty-plus years and help us to always count on you and your timing for our lives. Until you return, through Jesus I pray, amen.

A SEAL ON YOUR HEART

WEDDINGS! IS THERE a more beautiful or romantic time in a couple's life? Our own wedding was romantic to us but not exactly a showstopper like some of the ones we have performed for others. We got married in the preacher's living room, with his young daughter playing the wedding march on their piano (rather off key, as we recall), and the reception in their kitchen supervised by the preacher's wife. We had only about twenty people, mostly our immediate family. The ceremony came together quickly and cheaply because we didn't have any money, but it will always be special to us.

In Song of Solomon 8, Solomon talks about a seal over our heart and a seal on our arm and how such a seal represents love. When love is built correctly (in God's way), it is a blazing fire and can't be put out or quenched as long as God is at the center of it. We put seals on our fingers in the form of rings at our tiny wedding. A few years ago when we thought our love's fire had been quenched, we were ready to remove the seals on our fingers and walk away from each other.

But God intended for our love to last a lifetime. When we committed to each other, we also committed our love to God. And praise be to God! He had great plans for us. He helped us renew our love for Him and then for each other. We bought new seals for our fingers to signify a new commitment. They represented both a seal with God and with each other. The fire that Solomon talks about is blazing with Christ as the starter log. When we face difficulties in our marriages, sometimes we have to start completely over and rebuild with Christ as the foundation. It is possible. We did it and are living a blessed life because of it! When a relationship is rebuilt, even "many waters cannot quench" it.

We encourage you to honor the seals of your marriage and to stoke the fire of your love.

God's Blueprint: *Putting God's Word into Your Relationship*

Read the following scripture together out loud and talk a little about what the message behind the metaphors is.

SONG OF SOLOMON 8:6–7

PLACE ME LIKE A SEAL OVER YOUR HEART, LIKE A SEAL ON YOUR ARM; FOR LOVE IS AS STRONG AS DEATH, ITS JEALOUSY UNYIELDING AS THE GRAVE. IT BURNS LIKE BLAZING FIRE, LIKE A MIGHTY FLAME. MANY WATERS CANNOT QUENCH LOVE; RIVERS CANNOT SWEEP IT AWAY. IF ONE WERE TO GIVE ALL THE WEALTH OF ONE'S HOUSE FOR LOVE, IT WOULD BE UTTERLY SCORNED.

This is a great time to share sweet memories and even some funny ones, as you also think about your commitment to each other.

1. What stands out in your memory of your wedding? If you're unmarried, what do you hope your wedding will be like?

2. What do you think is significant about rings or other symbols of marriage?

3. What is the value you place on your love for each other? How do the pledges you made at your wedding with your rings remind you of your commitment even during difficult days?

Home Improvement: *Start Where You Are and Grow*

1. Write down some specific ways you can keep the fire of your love for each other stoked in your heart.
2. Tell your spouse your favorite thing he or she does to keep those fires burning.
3. List some ways you can help keep God at the center of your relationship.

Use the blank lines below to record some specific things you can begin doing in your relationship.

HER THOUGHTS

Tell me I'm pretty.

His Thoughts

_____

_____

_____

_____

_____

_____

_____

_____

_____

Team Building: *Grow Closer to Each Other as You Talk to God Together*

Read our prayers below out loud; then, using your own words, pray out loud and together. (You'll read these instructions every week—we don't want you to skip over this important time together.)

AL: Heavenly Father, what a blessing we have in Your being at the center of our relationship now. We came so close to blowing it and walking away, but by Your grace, mercy, and power, we now have a healthy relationship, and our fire of love burns warm and bright. I give You the praise for the good things in our lives and pray for our walk in You as we grow older. I pray this through Christ, amen.

LISA: Father, I am sorry that I fail in my attempts to love completely. So many times I build on temporary things instead of using You as our foundation. Thank You, Father, for allowing us to fail and then rebuild. Thank You for the fire that blazes within us as a couple. Please help us to continue to keep You as the foundation of our lives and in all that we do. Through Jesus I pray, amen.

WEEK 3

A PRAYERFUL HEART

PRAYER CHANGES EVERYTHING. Even if the change we ask for is not immediate, the hearts of those who pray are transformed. Sometimes we wonder if God even hears our prayers. When we don't see quick results, we start doubting He hears us. He does! But prayer has many facets. The answer to a request is only one part of a prayer. More important than our actual request is the fact that in the process of prayer, we humble ourselves to ask for help. An even more amazing part of this process is that we believe enough to ask. And in that process, we find ourselves building a relationship with the Creator of life! As we build a closer relationship with God, our relationship with each other grows stronger as well. We become more in tune with God and with each other. Wow, what a winning team we are building through prayer!

Even though our prayers are not always answered how we want them to be or when we want them to be, when we pray, we actually receive something greater than what we've asked for—we grow in the knowledge that we need the help of someone else greater than ourselves. This is what God looks for from all of us, a prayerful heart that seeks answers beyond our own limited scope. Prayer is one of the first things that helps develop a lifelong relationship with God, and it is the reason He asks us to pray to Him. Communication and asking for help is how you get to know and love your mate, as well as your family, and it is how you get to know your heavenly Father. Keep praying and know that He hears you—loud and clear—and that He is pleased with your heart of faith.

We encourage you to pray together to strengthen your relationship with God and with each other.

God's Blueprint: *Putting God's Word into Your Relationship*

As you read the scripture below, notice how *we are told to pray and the* results *that come from praying as instructed.*

PHILIPPIANS 4:6–7

DO NOT BE ANXIOUS ABOUT ANYTHING,

BUT IN EVERY SITUATION, BY PRAYER AND PETITION,

WITH THANKSGIVING, PRESENT YOUR REQUESTS

TO GOD. AND THE PEACE OF GOD,

WHICH TRANSCENDS ALL UNDERSTANDING,

WILL GUARD YOUR HEARTS AND YOUR

MINDS IN CHRIST JESUS.

Be honest with each other about any doubts you may have about prayer, and talk about how praying often and sometimes together can strengthen your faith.

1. How often do you pray to God?
2. Have you ever struggled with wondering whether or not He really listens to you or cares if you pray to Him?
3. Are you praying with your mate? Why is praying together something that could strengthen you both?

Home Improvement: *Start Where You Are and Grow*

1. What issues or topics do you need to lift up to the Father to ask His help or guidance with?
2. What are some of the benefits of spending time alone with God in prayer, and what are the benefits of praying together as a couple?
3. What do you like about hearing your mate pray out loud?

Record some of the things you need to pray about. Then you can refer to your notes later to see how you have grown and how God has intervened.

HER THOUGHTS

_____

_____

_____

_____

_____

_____

_____

_____

His Thoughts

_____

_____

_____

_____

_____

_____

_____

_____

Team Building: *Grow Closer to Each Other as You Talk to God Together*

Read our prayers below out loud; then, using your own words, pray out loud and together.

AL: Father, I am humbled to speak to You and share my innermost thoughts and fears. I don't feel judged by You, but I do feel bad when I realize I've let You down with poor decisions and behavior. Thanks for always being there for me, listening to me, and helping me be patient by awaiting your answers for my life. Through Jesus I pray, amen.

LISA: God, I don't always pray like I should, but I do want a deeper relationship with You. Teach me to long for those moments in Your throne room, where I can commune with You. In Jesus' name, amen.

LOVE IS THE GREATEST

THERE HAVE BEEN more poems and books written, songs performed, and movies made about love than any other subject. Human beings are obsessed with love, and there is an obvious reason why: it is the greatest emotion ever invented! Love motivates sacrifice, submission, protection, and meaning and has ever since people first showed up on our planet. Love motivates couples to take the leap of faith and decide to spend their lives together, and it has also allowed them to put the pieces back together when their dreams turn into nightmares.

The Bible says in 1 John 4:16 that God personifies love and that everything He does is motivated by this emotion. The Bible also says that God created all of us in His own image (Genesis 1:26), so it's easy to see why we are so eager to love and be loved. The problems come, however, because God is perfect in the way He loves, but we humans are not.

Love is the greatest motivation for building a great relationship, and as we grow in love, we build the foundations for staying healthy as a couple—even through years of trials and difficulties. We must continue to remind ourselves who we love, why we love, and how we can love better.

*We **encourage you*** to remember whose image you were created in, and when the tough times come, to look to Him and determine to grow in love.

God's Blueprint: *Putting God's Word into Your Relationship*

Read the following scripture together and out loud. Notice how powerful love must be if it is stronger even than faith and hope.

1 CORINTHIANS 13:13

AND NOW THESE THREE REMAIN: FAITH, HOPE AND LOVE. BUT THE GREATEST OF THESE IS LOVE.

Use the following questions to talk together about the effects of love on your relationship, and be lovingly honest about things that have tested your love.

1. Why do you think God ranks love above faith and hope?
2. How does God's love help you grow your love for your spouse?
3. When was the first time you knew you loved your mate?
4. What are some things that have tested your love up to this point?

Home Improvement: *Start Where You Are and Grow*

1. What are some things you can do to grow in love toward God or better receive His love for you?
2. What are some things you can do to help yourself grow in love in your relationships or better receive love from others?
3. Tell your loved one something you see in him or her that reflects God's image.

Record some of the ways you see God's love in your mate and ways you can live out the love God put in you, as you love your spouse. Look back later to see how you're doing.

HER THOUGHTS

_____

_____

_____

_____

_____

_____

_____

_____

_____

His Thoughts

_____

_____

_____

_____

_____

_____

_____

_____

_____

Team Building: *Grow Closer to Each Other as You Talk to God Together*

Read our prayers together and out loud, then use your own words to pray together about what God's love means to you.

AL: Heavenly Father, I am so thankful You are steeped in love and have shown me that I can love like you do. I freely admit I have so frequently failed to love like You do and have far too often failed to live up to the man You created me to be. I confidently ask for forgiveness, because You sent Your Son in love to make forgiveness possible. Help me love those around me like You love me. I pray this through the One who loved me when I was unlovable, Jesus, amen.

LISA: God, to know that You loved me when I was still an unforgiven sinner is an impossible thought for this human brain. But I know You did, because You sent me Your only Son as a sacrifice to save me. Wow! Many beautiful songs have been written about earthly love, but even more beautiful are the songs about Your love. Help my heart to sing of the heavenly love You give us each day. Teach me to love with that same love, even when it's not what I would choose to do. Thank You, Father, for the love that is always available and never conditional. In your sacrificed Son's name I pray, amen.

LOVE IS AND ISN'T . . .

ONE OF THE great mysteries pondered by people throughout the ages is, Is he or she *the one*? Are the feelings I have for this person true love that will last for a lifetime, even eternity? If you are old enough to have fallen in love, then you have been there and felt that!

For those of us who have taken the leap of love, we know that *trust* and *commitment* are just as important as how we *feel*. Love is so much more than a random or passing feeling; it has qualities and attributes that need to be discovered, nurtured, and grown.

The Bible is the best place to learn about the attributes of love, because God authored it as a love letter from Himself to all of humanity. The Bible describes in great detail where love comes from, what decisions must be made to cultivate it, and why it can ultimately deliver all people from the enemies of love. Even when human love fails, God offers the opportunity to renew love and rebuild something even stronger than before!

We encourage you to spend some time reflecting on love as not merely an emotion, but as a decision you make and a promise you keep. If you have felt burned by love, we encourage you to give it another chance by loving the way God defines love.

God's Blueprint: *Putting God's Word into Your Relationship*

Read the following scripture out loud and notice that love is defined by how we act, not how we feel.

1 CORINTHIANS 13:4–5

LOVE IS PATIENT, LOVE IS KIND. . . . IT IS NOT PROUD . . .
IT IS NOT SELF-SEEKING, IT IS NOT EASILY ANGERED.

Try to be honest and humble as you discuss the true attributes of love together.

1. How would you rank the love descriptions from the above verse, on a scale of 1–5 in importance to a relationship?
2. When you read this defining list of what love is and isn't, which attributes are strengths for you? Which do you need to work on?
3. What actions or behaviors are the opposite of attributes in this list? (Put these opposite descriptions in your own words.) Do you struggle with any of these attributes? Which ones?
4. How has failure to live out this love list hurt your relationships?

Home Improvement: *Start Where You Are and Grow*

1. What can you do to grow and cultivate your love list?
2. What can you do to help the one you love grow in this list?
3. Tell your loved one what his or her greatest strength is from this list.

Record your answers to the above questions. Next week, look back at this list and see what progress you've made.

HER THOUGHTS

_____

_____

_____

_____

_____

_____

_____

_____

His Thoughts

_____

_____

_____

_____

_____

_____

_____

_____

_____

Team Building: *Grow Closer to Each Other as You Talk to God Together*

Read our prayers together and out loud, then pray together about living out God's definition of love.

AL: Heavenly Father, I am very grateful that You have shown me what true love is. In my past, I have struggled with wondering whether the feelings I had were true love or simply a passing infatuation. You have anchored me with solid descriptions of what love is and isn't, and that model guides me to decide every day whom and why I love. I am blessed by Your consistency and ask forgiveness for my inconsistency. Help me be patient, kind, humble, selfless, slow to anger, and quick to forgive. I ask this in full confidence, because of Christ's example. In His name I pray, amen.

LISA: Lord, I am so humbled by Your love for me and Your providing me with a mate to love me here on this earth. I ask that You bless me with the ability to see what true love is and what love is not. I tend to confuse the two, but I know with your help I can be a lover who is patient and kind. I want you to remove the negative love barriers that hold me back from true, selfless love. Only through Jesus can I ask this prayer, amen.

LOVE DOES AND DOESN'T . . .

ONE OF THE great blessings of our married life thus far was the first six months, when we lived with Granny and Pa Robertson. We didn't have enough money to have our own place, so my grandparents went "old school" and allowed us to live in one of the extra bedrooms in their camp house on the Ouachita River. We gained the benefit of watching a couple who had been married almost fifty years. And while we weren't wise enough to know they were having an impact on our marriage, they definitely were! They weren't super affectionate and they didn't shower each other with gifts and platitudes, but they simply loved each other daily by *doing* for each other.

We learned from Granny and Pa that love is so much more than an emotion; it is a series of actions that are girded with feeling, commitment, and consistency. That doesn't sound super romantic, but the proof of love is actually in *doing* or sometimes *not doing* the things that come naturally. We are more affectionate than the generation before us, but we saw in them the great example of doing for each other in spite of difficulty, circumstance, and convenience. We have also learned that our natural reaction is not always conducive to love and that a good dose of self-control in *not* doing certain things can speak more love than something we do.

We encourage you to view love both as what you *do* and what you *don't* do. We also encourage you to love in such a way that generations beyond you will be blessed by what they see (or don't see) in you!

God's Blueprint: *Putting God's Word into Your Relationship*

Read the following scripture out loud and notice what love does *and* does not *do.*

1 CORINTHIANS 13:4–6

[LOVE] DOES NOT ENVY, IT DOES NOT BOAST. . . .
IT DOES NOT DISHONOR OTHERS, IT KEEPS NO
RECORD OF WRONGS. LOVE DOES NOT DELIGHT
IN EVIL BUT REJOICES WITH THE TRUTH.

As you work through the questions below, answer only for yourself—not your loved one.

1. Out of the six above descriptions of love's actions, most tell us what love does not do; only one tells us what love does do. Why do you think that is?
2. What does "rejoicing with the truth" mean? What does that look like as you love your mate?
3. Out of the five things love doesn't do, which are your strengths? Which are your weaknesses?
4. Out of the five things love doesn't do, what is your spouse best at not doing?

Home Improvement: *Start Where You Are and Grow*

1. What do you need to work on from this list to show more love?
2. Which one of these love actions is the weakest in your life, and what will you do to improve and show more love?

Be very specific and record what you plan not to do anymore, and how you hope your changes will grow your love.

HER THOUGHTS

_____

_____

_____

_____

_____

_____

_____

_____

His Thoughts

_____

_____

_____

_____

_____

_____

_____

_____

_____

Team Building: *Grow Closer to Each Other as You Talk to God Together*

Read our prayers together and out loud, then pray together in your own words about holding to God's dos and don'ts of love.

AL: My God and my Father, You have done so much to show Your love for all of humanity. I am sorry to say that a lot of what comes back to You, including things that come from me, have not been love at all. I have failed to live love so many times. I ask forgiveness for my shortcomings and humbly ask for wisdom to show more love to those I care about. Help me with self-control and with the ability to grow to be rich in love and mercy. Thank You for not holding my sins against me. I pray I will act like You and not hold the sins of those I love against them. I ask for this prayer through Jesus, my Great Mediator of Love, amen.

LISA: Jesus, God, and Holy Spirit, I humbly ask that the Trinity work in my life and produce a love language in me for the whole world to see. I pray that I can be an example to the world, to my brothers and sisters in Christ, and to my family. I want to leave a legacy of love for generations to come. Help me, Father God, to emulate Your love for me to my children, grandchildren, and my mate. Holy Spirit, please overshadow the thoughts that come from the evil one and help me to love unconditionally as the Father has done for me. Through the Name above All Names, Jesus, amen.

WEEK 7

NEVER SAY NEVER

WE CAN'T TELL you how many couples in crisis we have sat down with who begin their story with what we call the "always and never" description—but it is nearly every one of them! "She *always* puts me down!" "He *never* tells me he loves me!" "She *never* wants to have sex anymore!" "I think that I *never* actually loved him." You get the sad idea. These hyperboles, these exaggerations, can really hurt a relationship—and they're rarely true.

From our experience counseling other couples and from having our own marriage difficulties, we know to question the accuracy of *never* and *always*. We understand the emotion of crisis situations and why they feel as if there is no hope, but we also see that by affixing an unfixable status to a serious problem, we may be giving ourselves permission to walk away and allowing ourselves to see that as the only alternative. We believe this is a tactic of the evil one, as he attempts to wreck relationship after relationship.

Finding good solutions to serious problems often begins with understanding that *always* and *never* are seldom accurate descriptions. Relationships change, grow, morph, and twist into bad things but also into good things. All our behaviors change, sometimes positively and sometimes negatively, so it's important to be attuned to our behaviors and instincts and stay ahead of what can damage our relationships. We do this by allowing the only actual always and never to impact us—He who is immortal and unchanging, the almighty God. He gives us a few positive "always and nevers" in His Word that can help our relationships grow in hope rather than hopelessness. (See the scripture verse in this week's God's Blueprint.)

We encourage you to work on your perceived cases of *always* and *never,* and look to God's Word to learn what the true *always* and *never* really look like.

God's Blueprint: *Putting God's Word into Your Relationship*

Read the following scripture out loud and notice the always *and* never *that true love exhibits.*

1 CORINTHIANS 13:7–8

[LOVE] ALWAYS PROTECTS, ALWAYS TRUSTS,
ALWAYS HOPES, ALWAYS PERSEVERES.
LOVE NEVER FAILS.

As you talk through the questions below, be courageous enough to tell the truth about yourself.

1. Of the four *always* descriptions listed above, which is the easiest for you emulate? Which is the most difficult? Why?

2. Of the above descriptions, which does your loved one best emulate?

3. If love never fails, how do you explain relationship failures?

4. What challenges has your relationship persevered through? How does that give you hope?

Home Improvement: *Start Where You Are and Grow*

1. Which *always* from 1 Corinthians will you first try to implement in your relationship?
2. What behavior changes can you make that will ensure that love *never* fails in your relationship—even when you may not like each other very much?

Be specific as you record your answers to the above questions. Be sure to look back in a week or two to see how you're doing.

HER THOUGHTS

_____

_____

_____

_____

_____

_____

_____

_____

_____

HIS THOUGHTS

_____

_____

_____

_____

_____

_____

_____

_____

_____

Team Building: *Grow Closer to Each Other as You Talk to God Together*

Read our prayers below out loud; then, using your own words, pray out loud and together.

AL: Lord, You are our constant and unchanging hope in this ever-changing world. It is impossible for You to lie and sin, and because of that, I have hope that I can survive the dishonesty and sinfulness of our world and, sadly, of myself. I humbly ask forgiveness for my shortcomings and appeal to Your grace and mercy to lead me to a better and healthier attitude and life. I am grateful that Your mercies are new every morning and that Your love is steadfast and refreshing. Bless my relationship with the one I love and give us hope to always love You and never give up on You or us. I pray this through Jesus, my Lord and Savior, amen.

LISA: Father, I can't help but sing this prayer, "The steadfast love of the Lord never ceases." I rest in that promise, and I pray my love for You is never ceasing. I also pray, Father, that I can let trust, hope, perseverance, and love motivate me to a deeper relationship with You and a deeper relationship with the one I love. Only because You first loved me am I able to pray in Jesus' name, amen.

FORGIVE AND REMEMBER

S OMEONE ONCE SAID that three of the hardest words to say are "Please forgive me." It may be even harder to say "I forgive you." Yet harder still is actually *living* these words. How many arguments in your relationship have started with past hurt or point of conflict? Perhaps even a "forgiven" hurt? The last words of a fight are sometimes the first words in a new conflict.

Part of the problem may be the old slogan "Forgive and forget." Is that even possible? Maybe you can forget the time your spouse stepped on your foot or forget to go to the grocery store, but what about hurtful or sinful actions that betray or wound us deeply? Can we simply forget that those transgressions ever transpired? "I said the words and now we are moving on."

To be fair, the slogan probably comes from the book of Hebrews, where the Hebrews writer quotes Jeremiah of the Old Testament. Since God said He forgives and forgets, we can do the same, right?

How does the Creator of the Cosmos, the Listener of billions of thoughts and prayers forget anything? It would seem that even though God can remember everything, He chooses not to hold past sins against those whom He has forgiven. Thank you, God! God says that He would never bring up our past when dealing with our present. He remembers grace, but forgets sin and hurt.

We encourage you to follow God's winning formula, which allows Him to stay close to flawed human beings. We have experienced this forgiveness in our relationship, and we encourage you to build this important concept into your relationship as well.

God's Blueprint: *Putting God's Word into Your Relationship*

Read the following scriptures together and out loud and think about the amazing gift of forgiveness.

PSALM 130:3–4

IF YOU, LORD, KEPT A RECORD OF SINS, LORD,
WHO COULD STAND? BUT WITH YOU THERE IS FORGIVENESS,
SO THAT WE CAN, WITH REVERENCE, SERVE YOU.

HEBREWS 8:12

FOR I WILL FORGIVE THEIR WICKEDNESS
AND WILL REMEMBER THEIR SINS NO MORE.

Try to be honest as you talk about these important questions together.

1. Is it harder for you to ask for or to give forgiveness?
2. Is it harder to forgive others or to forgive yourself? Why?
3. How has bringing up past sins or wounds been detrimental to your relationship?

Home Improvement: *Start Where You Are and Grow*

1. Is there anything in your relationship that needs the words "Please forgive me" or "I forgive you"?
2. What about your heart needs to change so you can be better at receiving and giving forgiveness?
3. What has your mate forgiven you of that you are especially thankful for?

Be open enough to record your thoughts about what you've been forgiven for and how that should affect how you forgive others.

HER THOUGHTS

_____

_____

_____

_____

_____

_____

_____

_____

His Thoughts

_____

_____

_____

_____

_____

_____

_____

_____

_____

Team Building: *Grow Closer to Each Other as You Talk to God Together*

Read our prayers below out loud; then, using your own words, pray out loud and together about growing forgiveness in your relationship.

AL: Father, I am so thankful for the forgiveness You have offered me for my sins. I am so sorry I have hurt our relationship in the past and that I continue to fall short of Your perfect glory. I am grateful You live forgiveness every moment of my life and offer me fresh hope when I blow it. Thank You for the special one you have blessed me with and the opportunities to start fresh with her every day. You have blessed us with the forgiveness of past hurts that I never want to use against her or us. Forgive us when we aren't all we need to be. I pray this through Christ, my Savior, amen.

LISA: Father, I've had many shortcomings in my life, but You choose to remember them no more. Thank You, Father, that You do not bring them up each time I fall short. I pray I may do the same for my soul mate and for each relationship I have. Please help me to extend forgiveness and show grace and mercy as You have to me. I want to forgive and live that forgiveness each day of my life. Through Jesus I pray, amen.

Spirit Jam

ONE OF THE cornerstones of the Christian faith is the belief and expectation that when a person accepts Christ, God indwells that new Christian by sending His Holy Spirit to reside alongside his or her spirit—a built-in guide to prick our consciences and grow some great fruit through us!

We learned a lot about the Holy Spirit by watching the examples of Phil and Miss Kay when we were first married. They talk candidly about the first ten or twelve years of their relationship without the Holy Spirit, and it sounds like a disaster movie. Once Miss Kay became a Christian, then ultimately led Phil to the same place, a completely different relationship emerged. It took some time for old habits to die, but the more they relinquished control to the Holy Spirit, the more fruit began to grow in their lives and then affect their children and others around them.

One of the great things we have learned about the characteristics of the Spirit's fruit—which is detailed in the scripture following—is that these nine characteristics are not intended to be individually cherry-picked as we would like, but they are intended to be combined together and spread like jam. Our old friend Mac Owen calls it Spirit Jam, and he is right! If one of the characteristics of this fruit is not growing in us, then we are blocking the Holy Spirit and not getting the full effect of his fruit. We don't know about you guys, but we want the whole jam! We need the whole jam!

We encourage you to learn more about the Holy Spirit through Bible study and learning from others who know the Scriptures well. A great place to begin is with today's Bible passage.

God's Blueprint: *Putting God's Word into Your Relationship*

As you read the following scripture together, notice the amazing characteristics of the Spirit's fruit.

GALATIANS 5:22–26

BUT THE FRUIT OF THE SPIRIT IS LOVE, JOY, PEACE, FORBEARANCE, KINDNESS, GOODNESS, FAITHFULNESS, GENTLENESS AND SELF-CONTROL. AGAINST SUCH THINGS THERE IS NO LAW. THOSE WHO BELONG TO CHRIST JESUS HAVE CRUCIFIED THE FLESH WITH ITS PASSIONS AND DESIRES. SINCE WE LIVE BY THE SPIRIT, LET US KEEP IN STEP WITH THE SPIRIT. LET US NOT BECOME CONCEITED, PROVOKING AND ENVYING EACH OTHER.

Be honest about the needs in your life and generous in the praise of your spouse.

1. How does a relationship with God help our relationship with each other?

2. What Holy Spirit fruit seems to grow the best in you?

3. What Holy Spirit fruit is not growing in you as much as it should?

4. What gets in the way of allowing this growth in your relationship?

5. What Holy Spirit fruit is most evident in your loved one?

Home Improvement: *Start Where You Are and Grow*

Remember to be kind as you answer question number 2 below.

1. What can you do to help allow the Holy Spirit to grow the best fruit in you?
2. Ask your mate, What can I do to help allow the Holy Spirit to grow the best fruit in you?

Write out the characteristics of the Spirit's fruit that you want to grow in yourself and those you feel you are already growing in you.

HER THOUGHTS

_____

_____

_____

_____

_____

_____

_____

_____

His Thoughts

_____

_____

_____

_____

_____

_____

_____

_____

_____

Team Building: *Grow Closer to Each Other as You Talk to God Together*

Read our prayers below out loud; then, using your own words, pray together about growing the fruit of the Spirit in you and in the way you relate to each other.

AL: Heavenly Father, I am so thankful for the Holy Spirit you sent to live in me! The Spirit has grown so many blessings in me, and I am forever grateful. I'm sorry that I have blocked that growth at times, and I certainly know I have a lot more room to grow and more things I still need to "crucify" in my life so the Spirit can do more in me. Help me be a partner to my special lady, and help her grow so we can be a stronger couple. Thank You for blessing me with her and for blessing me daily with the Holy Spirit. Through Jesus I pray, with the help of the Spirit, amen.

LISA: Father God, You are my first, forever love. I pray that You continue to produce in me the fruit You know I so desperately need. I want to serve in Your image. Please Father, help me to water and feed this fruit and bless its growth in my life until the day You call me home to be with You. I pray that the mate You chose for me will be blessed by the fruit in my life. Thank You, God, for the Son You so freely gave so that we could have eternal life and a Holy Guide within us. Through Him, I pray, amen.

Communication

EASY LISTENING

THROUGH THE YEARS, we've had our share of songs that have spoken to our relationship. We don't have just one song that we consider "our song," but we have many because we have had so many different experiences through our years together. When we hear them, they remind us of our love or something we have overcome. Songs have the ability to capture a moment or a mood and sometimes amazingly speak straight to our hearts. Some songs actually make us sad and are not at all encouraging.

I'm sure you and your spouse have had conversations that were less than encouraging. The two of us certainly have. We believe that these are not of God. He tells us that our words should be like psalms and hymns—songs from the Spirit. Our words should be uplifting music to God and to the person to whom we are speaking. We are as guilty of not making beautiful music as anyone. And whose ears do our discouraging words usually fall to? Our beloved's!

There are times when we need to talk about things that are not pleasant, but even in these situations, we can use words to build up and not tear down our soul mates. When you need to discuss the ugly things in life, take a minute and access what you want the outcome to be. Take a minute and talk to the Father about it.

We encourage you to ask God before you begin a difficult conversation whether the conversation even needs to take place. If you conclude that it does, ask Him to guide your words and your heart and ask that His will prevail. Make music that is easy listening, not harsh and brutal!

God's Blueprint: *Putting God's Word into Your Relationship*

As you read the following scripture out loud, notice the emphasis this verse places on songs and music and how they relate to the Holy Spirit.

EPHESIANS 5:19–20

[SPEAK] TO ONE ANOTHER WITH PSALMS, HYMNS, AND SONGS FROM THE SPIRIT. SING AND MAKE MUSIC FROM YOUR HEART TO THE LORD, ALWAYS GIVING THANKS TO GOD THE FATHER FOR EVERYTHING, IN THE NAME OF OUR LORD JESUS CHRIST.

Honestly think about how you talk to each other and the impact your words and tone leave on the one you love.

1. What genre of music best describes your own conversation skills?
2. Do you and your loved one have a song that is "your song"? What is it? Is there another song that reminds you of your relationship?

3. Do you sometimes speak harshly to each other? If so, how can you improve this part of your communication?
4. How does seeing a conversation as a song help you to be more encouraging?

Home Improvement: *Start Where You Are and Grow*

1. What can you do differently to better encourage your mate?
2. What are some things you can do to be a better giver and receiver of encouragement?
3. Share a time your spouse used his or her words to encourage you. How did that make you feel?

Record some very specific things you plan to do differently to make your words more like sweet music.

HER THOUGHTS

_____

_____

_____

_____

_____

_____

_____

_____

His Thoughts

_____

_____

_____

_____

_____

_____

_____

_____

_____

Team Building: *Grow Closer to Each Other as You Talk to God Together*

Read our prayers together and out loud and then use your own words to pray together. (There's a reason we continually remind you to pray and read out loud: it's important that you participate in these steps together and that each of you can hear your mate's heart.)

AL: Heavenly Father, I am grateful for the songs You have put in me. The songs of forgiveness, redemption, love, and hope are now a part of my life because You sent Christ to save me. I pray I can speak those songs to my beloved and remove the harsh tones that so easily come from the part of me that hasn't fully surrendered to You. Forgive me for falling short and please continue to write new love songs for me to sing to You and to those I love on earth. In Christ's name, amen.

LISA: Father, I pray that as we grow in our marriage, You will put the correct words in my mouth regarding topics that need to be discussed. Remove words that might hurt or harm the one I love. Please Father, help me to be Your instrument to get any troublesome situations resolved to our benefit and to Your Glory, amen.

WEEK 11

BEST OF FRIENDS

WE HAVE MANY friends. Some are old (known for many years), some are new (in our travels, we meet some great people), some are Facebook friends (we've never met, just share stories), and then there's our best friend of all, each other. We love spending time with our couple friends, and we love spending time with our individual friends, but mostly, we love to spend time together. We love to travel, write books, watch TV, go to the beach, and just be in each other's presence. We haven't always had this type of relationship. In the past we have let things distract us from our focus on our relationship. We work hard to keep our relationship with each other first and foremost—second only to our relationship with Christ. We share our goals and dreams, we laugh together, and now we are approaching growing older together.

The key to any friendship is believing in each other and acting on that belief. Your commitment to maintaining and deepening a friendship with your mate will determine how healthy that relationship is. In the Bible, when James wrote about the balance between belief and action, he used the example of Abraham and how he felt and acted toward God. He said in James 2:22, "*His faith and his actions were working together, and his faith was made complete by what he did.*" In verse 23, James said, "*and he was called God's friend.*" What a great example for us in our relationship with God and also in our relationship with each other.

We encourage you to develop your friendship with each other so that your faith in each other and your actions toward each other work together for a deeper relationship.

God's Blueprint: *Putting God's Word into Your Relationship*

As you read the following scripture out loud and together, think about how it applies to your relationship.

ECCLESIASTES 4:9–12

TWO ARE BETTER THAN ONE, BECAUSE THEY HAVE A GOOD
RETURN FOR THEIR LABOR: IF EITHER OF THEM FALLS
DOWN, ONE CAN HELP THE OTHER UP. BUT PITY ANYONE
WHO FALLS AND HAS NO ONE TO HELP THEM UP. ALSO,
IF TWO LIE DOWN TOGETHER, THEY WILL KEEP WARM.
BUT HOW CAN ONE KEEP WARM ALONE? THOUGH ONE
MAY BE OVERPOWERED, TWO CAN DEFEND THEMSELVES.
A CORD OF THREE STRANDS IS NOT QUICKLY BROKEN.

Think about the place that friendship has in your relationship and how growing that friendship could affect your marriage.

1. Do you find it easy or difficult to make friends? Why is that?
2. Did your relationship start as friends or physical attraction? How has the friendship or attraction deepened or lessened?

What contributes to the growth or lack of growth in those relationships?

3. Would someone describe you as a friend of God by looking at your faith and actions?

4. How could deepening your relationship with God improve your friendship with each other?

Home Improvement: *Start Where You Are and Grow*

1. What are some things you can do to deepen your friendship with God?
2. What are some things you can do together to deepen your friendship with each other?
3. Tell your spouse about a time he or she acted like a true friend to you.

Record your thoughts on the part that friendship plays in your relationship and what you can do to be a better friend to your mate.

HER THOUGHTS

_____

_____

_____

_____

_____

_____

_____

_____

His Thoughts

_____

_____

_____

_____

_____

_____

_____

_____

_____

Team Building: *Grow Closer to Each Other as You Talk to God Together*

Read our prayers together and out loud, then using your own words, share your thoughts with each other and with God in prayer.

AL: Father, I respectfully call You my friend because I believe in You and strive to act on those beliefs. I fall short on my end and don't always act like a true friend, and for that I apologize and ask for forgiveness. Thank You for never failing our friendship. Thank You also for providing me with my best friend on earth and for putting us back together after our relationship fell apart. Our renewed friendship is now entwined with You to make us a cord not easily broken, and we praise you for that. Thank you for Christ, who made the ultimate sacrifice for us. Through Him I pray, amen.

LISA: Lord, thank You for the blessing of friends. We are so blessed to have so many. I am most thankful, Father, for the friendship of my best friend and love of my life. Thank You for showing me the way to a godly friendship and companionship. Help me to keep You at the center of our relationship. Because of the cross, amen.

IS TRUST EVEN POSSIBLE?

TRUST IS ONE of those things we all would love to have without reservation, but difficulties seem to make us wary of totally trusting in anyone or anything. These difficulties can range from the sickness of a child or death of a loved one to dishonesty in your marriage or death of your spouse. In each of these situations, you would love to totally trust in God or even your spouse, a friend, or a relative, but more times than not, you find yourselves holding back because of fear. We have gone through all these trials except the death of a spouse and have lost and rebuilt trust again and again. We can totally relate to the fear and mistrust that come about because of trials.

Through all our difficulties we have discovered that God is someone you can totally give that trust to without fear. Jesus' words to his disciples in John 14:1 have meant a lot to us during hard times: "*Do not let your hearts be troubled. Trust in God; trust also in me.*" You will still go through difficult situations, but He will always be there to comfort you, show you a different path, or even rescue you. You may not ever understand why you were faced with these trials, and that's when faith really kicks in.

It's very hard to put total trust in earthly beings because, as humans, we let one another down. We must work toward building and rebuilding trust with the love of our life, but it is imperative that we trust completely in our Heavenly Father. Recognize the source of your fear and let God take that fear and build complete trust in Him.

We encourage you to allow the trust in an unchangeable God to blend into your trust for each other.

God's Blueprint: *Putting God's Word into Your Relationship*

Read the following scripture out loud and notice what the writer says about what we should trust in and what we shouldn't.

PROVERBS 3:5–6

TRUST IN THE LORD WITH ALL YOUR HEART AND LEAN NOT ON YOUR OWN UNDERSTANDING; IN ALL YOUR WAYS SUBMIT TO HIM, AND HE WILL MAKE YOUR PATHS STRAIGHT.

Have the courage to examine your own trust issues and be kind toward your loved one as he or she does the same.

1. Is it easy or difficult for you to trust people? Why do you think that is?
2. How can trust in God help you build or rebuild trust in each other?
3. What is your greatest fear regarding your relationship? How can you help each other overcome that fear?
4. Share a time with your loved one when you felt safe with him or her, trusting that your mate had your back or would do the right thing.

Home Improvement: *Start Where You Are and Grow*

1. What are some reasons that trust has been difficult in your relationship?
2. What are some ways you can be more trustworthy?
3. What fears do you need to release to God, helping you trust in Him more?
4. Kindly tell your mate one thing he or she can do to help you trust him or her more.

Write down the central trust issues that you discovered in your discussion—especially recording specific things you can do to grow in trust toward God and your mate.

Her Thoughts

_____

_____

_____

_____

_____

_____

_____

_____

HIS THOUGHTS

_____

_____

_____

_____

_____

_____

_____

_____

_____

Team Building: *Grow Closer to Each Other as You Talk to God Together*

Read our prayers together and out loud, then pray together about the issue of trust in your relationship.

AL: Lord, You are the guide and path for my life, but I still fear and doubt because of my sin and the sin of others. I try to completely trust, but it is always a struggle. Help me give my fears to You and trust that You will always do what is best for me and for those I love. Help me be more like You and to trust in my ultimate salvation. Thank You for Christ and His sacrifice. In His name I pray, amen.

LISA: Father, sometimes I don't understand the "why" of earthly trials. Please help me to understand the "Who" in the heavenly realm that I can put total trust in. I ask that You help me build trust even more with my spouse as I seek to submit my heart to Your hands. Please forgive me when I break that trust with You and also with the ones I love most here on earth. Create in me a pure heart and a life that glorifies You. Through Jesus, with the help of his Spirit, I pray, amen.

WITHOUT FEAR AND WITHOUT SHAME

WE HAVE EXPERIENCED shame and fear in our marriage because one or both of us went through periods where we were not living for Christ and allowed sin to rule our hearts. We can't change our past, but we can change how we deal with it and how we shape our future together.

The very first man and the very first woman also happened to be the very first husband and the very first wife. They had the ideal setting for their marriage, as they lived in a beautiful garden without clothes, without a former boyfriend or girlfriend to compare themselves to, without mothers-in-law to criticize, and the best "without" of all—without sin! That is, until sin came calling through Satan's invitation to eat the forbidden fruit. After they disobeyed God and ate of the *one* tree He told them to avoid, their eyes were opened and they immediately felt the emotion of shame because they were running around without any clothes on. Their next emotion was fear because they knew they had disobeyed God and had chosen to become their own gods. You can read all about it in Genesis 3.

Shame and fear were originally born out of sin, and unfortunately for all of humanity, that cycle of sin-shame-fear has repeated itself in relationships right up to this very second. Thank goodness for the hope we have in Christ so that we no longer have to live in shame and fear. We might say that the opposites of shame and fear are confidence and courage. Only when we allow God to remove fear and shame from our relationships can we be filled with His confidence and courage. Fear and shame cannot co-exist with these two gifts from God.

We encourage you to live unashamed and unafraid. You can do this through honesty, forgiveness, and trust in the God who saves, cleanses, and renews. As a couple, we live by John's words in 1 John 2:28–29: "And now, dear children, continue in him, so that when he appears we may be confident and unashamed before him at his coming."

God's Blueprint: *Putting God's Word into Your Relationship*

Read the scripture below together and notice what we have to do in order for God to deliver us.

PSALM 34:4–5

I SOUGHT THE LORD, AND HE ANSWERED ME;
HE DELIVERED ME FROM ALL MY FEARS.
THOSE WHO LOOK TO HIM ARE RADIANT;
THEIR FACES ARE NEVER COVERED WITH SHAME.

Use these questions to honestly share together how you can live shame-free.

1. Can you remember the first time you felt shame or fear? Share that time with your loved one.
2. What are the negatives that come from shame and fear in a relationship?
3. How does a healthy relationship with God help take away shame and fear in your life?

Home Improvement: *Start Where You Are and Grow*

1. What things or attitudes have you allowed to shame you?
2. What can you do to help remove shame and fear from the one you love?
3. What can you do together to bring confidence and courage into your relationship?
4. Share a time your mate gave you courage or confidence.

This week, record the things that make you fearful or cause you to feel ashamed. Then write down what you learned from your discussion about how you might overcome these negative emotions.

HER THOUGHTS

_____

_____

_____

_____

_____

_____

_____

_____

His Thoughts

_____

_____

_____

_____

_____

_____

_____

_____

_____

Team Building: *Grow Closer to Each Other as You Talk to God Together*

Read our prayers together and out loud, then pray together about how you can remove shame from your relationship.

AL: Heavenly Father, You are the author of confidence and the remover of fear. Your perfect love casts out fear, and I am so thankful I can confidently rely on You when I don't trust myself. You are truly greater than my heart, and because of my relationship with You, I can live unafraid and unashamed. Please help me to live this way and encourage that same heart in my beloved. Help me to be a good receiver of her honesty and, even when the trust is hard to hear, to never tear her down but build her up by my words and actions. I pray this prayer in anticipation of the coming of Christ, to Your glory, amen.

LISA: Lord, you know that honesty has not always been a character trait for me. So many times the sins of others or our own sin puts us in a place of shame and guilt. Thank You, Father, that I can live without shame and guilt-free because of Christ. I want to be totally honest with my mate and totally honest with You, my Savior. Continue to help me build godly character traits in my life. In our Redeemer and Your Son's name I pray, amen.

A CAUTIONARY TALE

WHEN WE STARTED giving our testimony of what God had done to save our marriage, people often told us we needed to write a book about our story. Eventually we did write that book, *A New Season*, in hopes that people who were hurting could discover what we did to overcome extreme difficulties in our relationship and how to apply these lessons to their own relationships. We also hope that our story is a cautionary tale for young couples about what *not* to do early in their relationship. The only extraordinary thing about us is that we allowed God to intervene and guide us.

The Bible is full of people who did extraordinary things on God's behalf, and reading about them has inspired us to believe that we also can do great things for God. King David in 1 and 2 Samuel was one of those inspirational guys whose many mighty deeds teach us a lot about God's power in our lives, but perhaps the most important lesson we learn from him is what not to do: in this cautionary tale, we see that David did not guard and protect his faithfulness.

David had a full-blown affair with the wife of one of his soldiers and then murdered the man to cover up the affair after she became pregnant. The whole thing played out like a bad Lifetime movie. If you read 2 Samuel 11, you can see that it all started with David's being somewhere he shouldn't have been, looking at something he shouldn't have looked at, and then ignoring the warnings that he should have listened to. After David had the woman's husband murdered, he married her to make it seem that the situation was honorable. But the deception was now in place, and it was more than a year before David was challenged by God's prophet and he finally realized his sin.

If you want to read David's anguished response to God, check out Psalm 51. He ultimately got it right, but he paid a heavy price within his family from that point forward. Ironically, his own son wrote words in Proverbs 16 that could have saved David and his family from his terrible fall.

We encourage you to learn from David's mistakes and to live cautiously in relation to those who would destroy your relationship.

God's Blueprint: *Putting God's Word into Your Relationship*

Read the following scripture together and think about the advice it gives on how to stay away from trouble.

PROVERBS 16:17–18
THE HIGHWAY OF THE UPRIGHT AVOIDS EVIL;
THOSE WHO GUARD THEIR WAYS PRESERVE
THEIR LIVES. PRIDE GOES BEFORE DESTRUCTION,
A HAUGHTY SPIRIT BEFORE A FALL.

Open your Bibles together and read David's story.

1. How can you relate today to David's situation and mindset in 2 Samuel 11:1–4, even though it happened many, many years ago?
2. What are some areas that need to be put under guard in your relationship to avoid potential falls?
3. How do pride and a haughty spirit lead to falling?

Home Improvement: *Start Where You Are and Grow*

1. What are some practical things that each of you can do to help guard the other?
2. What are some commitments you can make and keep to help insure that you guard your faithfulness to God and to your significant other?
3. Share with your loved one a specific way that he or she has shown faithful commitment to your relationship.

Thoughtfully and honestly write down things that you need to avoid and guard against so you will stay faithful to your loved one.

HER THOUGHTS

_____

_____

_____

_____

_____

_____

_____

_____

_____

_____

_____

_____

_____

_____

_____

_____

_____

_____

Team Building: *Grow Closer to Each Other as You Talk to God Together*

Read our prayers together and out loud, then pray together about avoiding potentially unrighteous relationships.

AL: God, I want to humble myself before You and ask You to remove any haughtiness that exists in me, so I will recognize traps set before me. I am grateful that You offer us healing and hope from falls, but I don't want my love to have to deal with hurt caused by me. Please help me to go to and live in places that are honest and holy, and to guard my eyes from things that lead me to evil and impurity. Help me look for and heed the warnings of friends and Your servants as I live my daily life. Forgive me for falling short and strengthen me to be like You. In Christ I have hope, and I pray through him, amen.

LISA: Father, I want to thank you for your forgiveness. Even when we continue down the same dangerous road, You still send Your people, our friends, to warn us and bring us back. You are our great Redeemer, our path to righteousness. Help me to follow You all the days of my life and to help others on the road to heaven. Take away my pride when I think more highly of myself than I should and don't heed Your warnings. Because of Jesus' life and death, through Him I pray, amen.

Forgiveness

HOW MANY TIMES MUST I FORGIVE?

HAVE YOU EVER grown weary of doing the right thing when someone consistently responds with the wrong thing? Do you find yourself saying, "I can't take this anymore!" or "How long am I expected to keep this up?" We have, and we imagine that you have been there too.

Out of the many questions Jesus' disciples asked him that are recorded in the gospels, one of the most practical is asked by Peter in Matthew 18:21. In typical Peter style, he asks the question and then provides a potential answer. "Lord, how many times shall I forgive my brother or sister who sins against me? Up to seven times?" Wow, Peter, seven whole times! I bet Mrs. Peter would have loved that generous offer. Jesus answered with a specific number, but He was actually teaching a lifestyle principle. Jesus answered, "I tell you, not seven times, but seventy-seven times." Some versions actually interpret the answer to be "seventy times seven," which would be 490 times! We know it's not the exact number that matters because Jesus follows up with a parable about a guy who received forgiveness for a large debt but wouldn't offer forgiveness for a small debt. He concluded in Matthew 18:35 that God forgives us without counting and we should do the same—that's a lifestyle principle!

In relationships, especially a lifelong marriage, there will be ample opportunities to forgive and be forgiven. We don't want a limited count that runs out. From the little, stupid things we do to the big, ugly things, forgiveness is the only consistent answer for repairing our shortcomings and renewing our relationships ourselves. If we really are going to live a lifetime of forgiveness, we must live the short phrase describing love in 1 Corinthians 13 and "keep no record of wrongs"—and, we would add, no record of rights either! Choose to put your tab on the cross of Christ, where no one's counting but everyone's forgiven.

We encourage you to be open-hearted and forgiving toward each other. Be patient when your loved one does the same wrong thing over and over, and work to forgive.

God's Blueprint: *Putting God's Word into Your Relationship*

As you read the following scripture together and out loud, hear them in regard to yourself rather than the other person.

COLOSSIANS 3:13
BEAR WITH EACH OTHER AND FORGIVE
ONE ANOTHER IF ANY OF YOU HAS A GRIEVANCE
AGAINST SOMEONE. FORGIVE AS THE LORD
FORGAVE YOU.

As you work through the following questions, focus on how you need to change, not how your loved one needs to change.

1. In the scripture you just read, what guideline does Jesus give us for how we should forgive others?
2. Have you ever been frustrated enough in your relationship to think, "How long can I put up with this?" or "How many times am I going to have to deal with this issue?" How does what Jesus said help you deal with that frustration?
3. How does bearing with each other help pave the way for forgiveness in your relationship?
4. Why does Paul remind us of our forgiveness by God in this challenge?

Home Improvement: *Start Where You Are and Grow*

1. How can you better exhibit a lifestyle of forgiveness, especially to your mate?
2. What list of grievances do you need to delete from your short- and long-term memory?
3. Share a time when each of you felt the other's forgiveness. How did that forgiveness make you feel?

Dig deep into your heart and write down some things you still need to forgive about your loved one, then ask God to help you overcome any resentment or bitterness you may feel.

HER THOUGHTS

_____

_____

_____

_____

_____

_____

_____

_____

_____

His Thoughts

_____

_____

_____

_____

_____

_____

_____

_____

_____

Team Building: *Grow Closer to Each Other as You Talk to God Together*

Read our prayers below out loud; then, using your own words, pray to-gether about growing forgiveness in your hearts and actions.

AL: My God of love and forgiveness, I thank You for not counting my list of wrongs and comparing them to my list of rights. I know my scales wouldn't balance, and I know You couldn't be with me if I tried to overcome my wrongs without Your grace. I am grateful for the cleansing of my sins, and I continually live a life of repentance before You and with the love of my life. Please help me continue to live a life of forgiveness and keep no record of other's wrongs or rights, but rather take each day, each moment, as it comes and live as You would have me live. I am blessed in Christ and pray in His name, amen.

LISA: Lord God, I have sinned many times against other people and others have sinned against me, but nothing compares to the number of times I've sinned against You. You don't keep a running tally, and You tell us in Hebrews 8:12 that You remember them no lon-ger. Wow! Father, again, I am amazed at Your love for me. The same forgiveness and forgetfulness that You demonstrate to me, I want to have for others, especially the love of my life. Help me, Lord. You know I'm weak. Remind me of Your forgiveness each day. Through Jesus, amen.

BUILDING YOUR LEGACY

I N OUR FAMILY, hunting is a big part of our legacy. Because of a passion Phil's dad had for hunting, especially duck hunting, the legacy was passed to his sons. Phil was uniquely gifted to make duck calls that sound just like a duck, so that passion became even stronger, and he passed on to his sons a love for hunting and the great outdoors. All the boys have varying degrees of skills and different loves for different types of hunting, but the legacy now rolls on to our children and nephews and nieces. One of our sons-in-law carries that same passion and will probably keep the legacy going through our branch for generations to come. While hunting is a big deal for us, there is a much more important legacy we are passionate about.

What type of spiritual legacy are you a part of? Were your folks Christians? How about your grandparents or great-grandparents? Some of you come from a long lineage of Christians, but we also know from working with many couples that some of you are starting the Christian legacy yourself. Whatever category you find yourself in, this question is for you: What legacy are you leaving for your family? What will be said of you by future generations of your family?

We were blessed with a spiritual legacy going back several generations, and we want to carry on that legacy by encouraging our children, grandchildren, and great-grandchildren to know, love, and put their total faith in God. For this to happen, faith has to be a way of life for us first.

We encourage you to think about and honestly observe what your family witnesses in you. Is your legacy worth repeating in generations to come? If not, break the curse and begin a new spiritual legacy today.

God's Blueprint: *Putting God's Word into Your Relationship*

Read the following scripture out loud and notice who passed on the faith to a future generation and how that made him feel.

3 JOHN 1:3–4

IT GAVE ME GREAT JOY WHEN SOME BELIEVERS
CAME AND TESTIFIED ABOUT YOUR FAITHFULNESS TO
THE TRUTH, TELLING HOW YOU CONTINUE TO WALK
IN IT. I HAVE NO GREATER JOY THAN TO HEAR THAT
MY CHILDREN ARE WALKING IN THE TRUTH.

Use this time to share with each other the impact the generations before you have had on you—for good or for bad.

1. What traditions have been passed down in your families?
2. What new things do you hope to pass down to the generations to come?
3. Are there any legacies you want to end with your generation?
4. What do you hope generations after you will accomplish?

Home Improvement: *Start Where You Are and Grow*

1. What are some things you can do to ensure that a positive spiritual legacy is left after you are gone?
2. What do you want to accomplish during your life to pass on to future generations?
3. Share with each other at least one quality you inherited from your family of origin that you appreciate and want to pass on to future generations.

Write out the legacies you want to pass on, and be specific in what you can begin doing now to build those legacies in your life.

HER THOUGHTS

_____

_____

_____

_____

_____

_____

_____

_____

His Thoughts

_____

_____

_____

_____

_____

_____

_____

_____

_____

Team Building: *Grow Closer to Each Other as You Talk to God Together*

Read our prayers below out loud; then pray together about the legacy you want to leave and how to make sure you do.

AL: Father, I am so grateful for the family legacy that has been passed down to me of love and appreciation for You and the knowledge of the good news of Your Son, Jesus. I pray that You give me the wisdom and vision to pass along what I have learned and to improve on the things handed down to me. I pray that generations from now, the Robertson name will stand for integrity, grace, and a love of biblical truth. Through Jesus I pray as I eagerly await his coming, amen.

LISA: Lord, help me to take a deep look inside my family and find out what others are seeing in our lives. If it's not our Christian values, then Lord, give me the strength and endurance to help us change together. Create in me a pure heart, a clean life, and a moral standard for generations to follow. Always through Jesus, I ask, amen.

MONSTER-IN-LAW OR MOTHER-IN-LOVE

MISS KAY IS one of the best mothers-in-law (mothers-in-love) that God has created. She does not take sides, and neither of us can get away with anything. She had four sons but always wanted a few daughters and now through marriage has four daughters. She was still raising Jase, Willie, and Jep when we got married. So it wasn't like she was an older, wiser grandmother type, but she always seemed to have the right touch of encouragement and wisdom during our early, turbulent years of marriage. We both felt comfortable going to her when we struggled, which is unusual in many families because it is so easy for mothers-in-law to choose their child's side in an argument or difficult situation.

God set a great relationship truth in His standard for marriage in Genesis 2:24 by encouraging husbands and wives to leave their mothers and fathers and cling to each other. In other words, when marriage occurs, dependence on parents is severed and an interdependence with each other is established in a brand-new family. This doesn't mean you won't be expected to honor your parents and have a respectful, loving relationship with them.

We are now in-laws ourselves, and we want our sons-in-law to be "in love" with us as well. We try not to interfere in their matters unless asked. It's hard, though, because they are married to our daughters, and they discipline our grandchildren. We use Miss Kay as our example and continue to read the words of Ruth as our guide (see this week's God's Blueprint). If we get in their business, we are creating discord between our families. We want our daughters' husbands to feel about us as Ruth did about Naomi. We want love, trust, and unity to be firmly planted in their immediate family unit. We won't always be there with them, but we want them to always be there for their family.

We encourage you not to give your in-laws any reasons to feel "monstrous" toward you, and when you become parents-in-law yourselves, don't be monsters-in-law but follow the example set in the book of Ruth and be "in-laws-in-love"!

God's Blueprint: *Putting God's Word into Your Relationship*

As you read the following scripture together, take note of how Ruth's commitment to her mother-in-law was demonstrated.

RUTH 1:16–17

BUT RUTH REPLIED, "DON'T URGE ME TO LEAVE YOU OR TO TURN BACK FROM YOU. WHERE YOU GO I WILL GO, AND WHERE YOU STAY I WILL STAY. YOUR PEOPLE WILL BE MY PEOPLE AND YOUR GOD MY GOD. WHERE YOU DIE I WILL DIE, AND THERE I WILL BE BURIED. MAY THE LORD DEAL WITH ME, BE IT EVER SO SEVERELY, IF EVEN DEATH SEPARATES YOU AND ME."

Honestly and kindly answer the questions below as you think seriously about your in-laws.

1. What kind of relationship do you have with the family of your mate?
2. Have you ever expressed your appreciation to your mate's parents for raising your mate and giving him or her to you?
3. How important is it to each of you that there is a strong bond with each other's families?
4. Tell your loved one what you appreciate most about his or her family.

Home Improvement: *Start Where You Are and Grow*

1. What can you both commit to do as a couple that will help each other have better relationships with your families?
2. What is your plan for dealing with additions to your families with sons- or daughters-in-law?

Think about what you can do to improve your relationship with your in-laws and about things they do that you want to emulate and things you'd like to do differently.

HER THOUGHTS

_____

_____

_____

_____

_____

_____

_____

_____

His Thoughts

_____

_____

_____

_____

_____

_____

_____

_____

_____

Team Building: *Grow Closer to Each Other as You Talk to God Together*

Read our prayers together and out loud, then pray about your relationship with your in-laws and how you can make it more loving.

AL: Lord, what a blessing it is to have such a great relationship with our families. I humbly ask forgiveness for the times when I have not been generous in my relationship with my in-laws and pray that I will work to be selfless in my approach to my sons-in-law and their relationships with my daughters. Help me to be a great example for them to follow as I strive to be like You every day. I ask this prayer in Jesus' name, amen.

LISA: Father, I pray you touch all our relationships but especially those in our in-law family. Guide me to be the godly example I should be in these relationships. Thank You for the example of Ruth and Naomi. I ask for Your hand to be on me in all these situations. Because You are the Great Redeemer, I pray in Your sacrificed Son's name, Jesus, amen.

WEEK 18

BEAUTY IS ONLY SKIN DEEP

WRINKLES, LAUGH LINES, age spots, crow's feet—these are all signs that our beauty is fading. What do these things represent? Age! And with age comes . . . ? Wisdom! What does God think about external beauty? He says it's fleeting. "But a woman who fears the Lord is to praised." (Proverbs 31:30)

Both men and women who fear the Lord are the most good-looking of all—no matter their ages. Inward beauty radiates to our outward appearance. There are a lot of people who look good on the outside but have very ugly hearts.

Two examples of biblical inner beauty are seen in an ancient woman and man. In 1 Peter 3, Peter describes Sarah, the wife of Abraham, as a woman with the inner beauty of a quiet and submissive spirit who loved her man and wasn't at all concerned about the outer stuff. She did have a kid at ninety, you know!

Joseph is another example, as he was described in Genesis 39 as being well built and handsome. Yet the true beauty of this man was seen in his decision to honor God with his body and not succumb to the advances of his boss's wife. It was also seen in his heart of forgiveness toward his brothers years later when he could have had vengeance against them. These honorable qualities are much more important than a reflection in a mirror.

We encourage you to look in the mirror, really look, and focus on the area behind your eyes where your spirit resides. That is what God sees, and it's the portal to all your beauty.

God's Blueprint: *Putting God's Word into Your Relationship*

Read the following scripture out loud and together and think about how you can be more beautiful on the inside.

PROVERBS 31:30

CHARM IS DECEPTIVE, AND BEAUTY IS FLEETING;

BUT A WOMAN WHO FEARS THE LORD IS TO BE PRAISED.

Don't be afraid to be honest about your physical appearance versus your inward beauty. This discussion will set you on the path to a more beautiful (handsome) you.

1. How important is physical appearance in your relationship?
2. How important is it to each of you to get positive, encouraging feedback and compliments on your physical appearance?
3. Do you feel your physical appearance dominates too much of your thoughts, worries, or fears?
4. What qualities of inner beauty do you see in each other?

Home Improvement: *Start Where You Are and Grow*

1. Talk together about ways each of you can dedicate more time and effort to growing your inner spirit and inner beauty.
2. Tell your loved one what he or she can do to encourage you to grow in your inner beauty.

Write down beautiful characteristics you already possess, as well as ones you want to cultivate. Then write down what you'll do to grow these beautiful, new characteristics in yourself.

HER THOUGHTS

_____

_____

_____

_____

_____

_____

_____

_____

His Thoughts

_____

_____

_____

_____

_____

_____

_____

_____

_____

Team Building: *Grow Closer to Each Other as You Talk to God Together*

Read our prayers together and out loud, then pray that your hearts will become more and more beautiful.

AL: Lord, I am grateful that You have blessed us with a certain amount of physical appeal, but I am far more grateful for the humility You have grown in our hearts and for helping our hearts to want to please You and look out for each other. I am so thankful for my forever love's commitment to growing her inner beauty; she radiates it more every year, and every year she grows to be more like You. Thank You for the beauty of Christ's sacrifice on that ugly cross. Through Him I pray, amen.

LISA: Father, You know that I sometimes focus too much on my outer appearance and struggle with remembering where my real beauty lies. Show me, Father. Help me listen to Your Word and learn what characteristics You call beautiful. Help me to be a woman who is praised because of my love for You! Because of the cross that takes my burdens and sins, I pray through Jesus. Amen.

THE SECRET TO BEING CONTENT

I N OUR OWN thirty-plus years together, our material circumstances have varied greatly. We have experienced times of need and times of plenty, and we have discovered that contentment with the blessings we *do* have—as well as persistent reliance on the Lord whether we have much or little—has been the sustaining factor through it all.

When we were first married and were helping start Duck Commander, we had very little, as far as material things go, for the first couple of years. But we were content. As time went by, we spent twenty-two years in full-time ministry and always struggled to make ends meet, but we were content. Now we are on a hit television show and have written several books and are known by millions of people, and we are still content. How do any of us survive the lean times? How do we not become conceited when we are riding high? The answer is the same for both questions: the realization that because of Him and His power, we can find contentment in all things. You can and you will make it if you learn this important lesson. Don't shut out the almighty power of God. He gives us the strength and endurance to run with turkeys and soar with eagles!

We encourage you not to count your blessings by how much you have externally but to learn to be content—no matter what the circumstances.

God's Blueprint: *Putting God's Word into Your Relationship*

As you read the following scripture out loud, think about your material situation—are you in need or do you have plenty?—then notice what the writer says about how you are to feel, no matter what.

PHILIPPIANS 4:11–13

I HAVE LEARNED TO BE CONTENT WHATEVER THE CIRCUMSTANCES. I KNOW WHAT IT IS TO BE IN NEED, AND I KNOW WHAT IT IS TO HAVE PLENTY. I HAVE LEARNED THE SECRET OF BEING CONTENT IN ANY AND EVERY SITUATION, WHETHER WELL FED OR HUNGRY, WHETHER LIVING IN PLENTY OR IN WANT. I CAN DO ALL THIS THROUGH HIM WHO GIVES ME STRENGTH.

Talk honestly about the questions below.

1. How do you balance ambition and contentment?
2. What are some of your fears and worries about where you are right now materially?
3. How do you encourage each other to be content and trust in God when things are tough?
4. Tell your loved one at least one thing he or she does to help you be content.

Home Improvement: *Start Where You Are and Grow*

1. What positive things have you learned about your relationship when you endured something difficult?
2. What can you do as a couple to stay focused on God's power, rather than your own, in times of plenty or need?

Write about what makes you feel content—and be honest. Write about areas you need to grow in and how you can do that.

HER THOUGHTS

_____

_____

_____

_____

_____

_____

_____

_____

HIS THOUGHTS

_____

_____

_____

_____

_____

_____

_____

_____

_____

Team Building: *Grow Closer to Each Other as You Talk to God Together*

Read our prayers together and out loud, then pray together about growing contentment in your lives.

AL: Father, You are the only source of true strength for my life. When I rely on my own abilities or strength, I always end up failing. Forgive me for my arrogance and weakness when I try to do it myself. Thank You for blessing us with plenty and sustaining us when we are in need. May I always find contentment in looking to You and the ultimate blessing of eternal life with You, as I continue to run the race You have marked out for us. Through Christ I pray, amen.

LISA: In my weakness, Father, You are my strength. Teach me to be content no matter my circumstances and to draw from Your strength rather than trying to rely on my own feeble feats. In Jesus' name, amen.

I'M LOOKING OUT FOR YOU

O NE OF THE first things most of us were guilty of is selfishness. You know this is true by watching small children on a playground or in a room full of toys. You rarely ever see them sharing or offering other children a toy or a ride, but almost always see them claiming something as theirs and refusing to share until Mom steps in. This shows how ingrained selfishness is, and if it grows along with a child into adulthood, it can be very difficult on a relationship.

Perhaps the greatest quality exhibited by Jesus Christ was his selflessness. When you read the account of his ministry in the four gospels (Matthew, Mark, Luke, and John), you see Jesus consistently lifting others up and not once doing anything selfish. The last selfless act He performed was allowing Himself to be brutalized and crucified even though He was completely innocent of any wrongdoing. This attitude goes against human nature and is the gold standard for successful relationships. Jesus was able to empathize with all of humanity in spite of the fact that everyone He was trying to help had selfish motives, including those closest to him.

We believe that striving for empathy and selflessness is the key to having a great relationship with anyone you love, especially your mate. Just think about how you would change if every action you took was weighted by the thought "How will this affect my mate?" It would be very hard to have major conflict if we even just *tried* to think like this! There is no doubt that our relationship has had the most growth when we were working to apply this principle in our daily living. We realize this goes against what is natural to all of us, but that is what spiritual transformation is all about—replacing the natural with the spiritual to become more like Christ.

We encourage you, and we implore you to work on thinking about how your actions and reactions will affect your loved one. You will be amazed at what will happen in your relationship.

God's Blueprint: *Putting God's Word into Your Relationship*

Read the scripture below out loud and together, and notice what the opposite of "selfish ambition" and "vain conceit" are.

PHILIPPIANS 2:3–5

DO NOTHING OUT OF SELFISH AMBITION OR VAIN CONCEIT. RATHER, IN HUMILITY VALUE OTHERS ABOVE YOURSELVES, NOT LOOKING TO YOUR OWN INTERESTS BUT EACH OF YOU TO THE INTERESTS OF THE OTHERS. IN YOUR RELATIONSHIPS WITH ONE ANOTHER, HAVE THE SAME MINDSET AS CHRIST JESUS.

As you share your thoughts, focus on what you need to do differently (not on what your loved one needs to do).

1. Why is it so difficult to be unselfish and not vain?
2. What are some things you see in Christ's attitude that would be good to apply to yourself and your relationship?
3. How would your relationship change if you were able to apply this principle to all your actions?
4. Share with your loved one a specific time he or she was selfless and put you first.

Home Improvement: *Start Where You Are and Grow*

1. What are you as a couple doing well—in terms of being selfless—in your relationship?
2. What areas do you personally need to work on in order to be selfless?
3. What are some specific attitudes and actions you need to change in order to have the mindset of Jesus Christ?

Record some of the things you talked about in your discussion that apply to you personally, in order for you to become more Christlike and more focused on the needs of your loved one.

HER THOUGHTS

_____

_____

_____

_____

_____

_____

_____

_____

_____

His Thoughts

_____

_____

_____

_____

_____

_____

_____

_____

_____

Team Building: *Grow Closer to Each Other as You Talk to God Together*

Read our prayers together and out loud, then pray your own prayers together, with becoming more selfless in mind.

AL: Father, when I think about how much You love me, in spite of my shortcomings, I am simply blown away. Thank You so much for showing me empathy and compassion whether I am doing well or doing poorly. I thank You for Your Son, Jesus, and that He become one of us. Because He was one of us, we now know we can be more like Him and have amazing relationships here on earth despite our weaknesses. I pray through Him, amen.

LISA: Lord, You show us a perfect example of what it means to be selfless, to show empathy, to feel sympathy. You know my heart, so You know I'm not always a good example of these qualities. Father, give me Your spirit of selflessness, Your heart of empathy, and Your selfless love through sympathy. How I long to put my soul mate first in my life and have the selflessness toward him that You show toward all humanity. Thank You Father for the gift of a man to love and the blessing of being loved here on earth. With the help of the Spirit, through the name above names, Jesus, amen.

FORGIVENESS TAKES TWO

I N OUR BOOK *A New Season*, we were very open about how we've hurt and harmed each other in the thirty-plus years we've known each other. At different times in our lives, we were so steeped in sinfulness that we just didn't seem to care who got in the way of our pleasure. Now we both regret those hurts and have come to the realization that we can't do one thing to change our past behavior. But we can live every day differently than we did in the past and change our behavior and attitudes—and thus their consequences in our lives.

Has someone sinned against you so badly you thought you could never forgive him or her? Surely you couldn't forgive the person unless he or she begged for it, and maybe even then you thought the offense was too grave a sin to forgive. But God teaches us again and again in His Word that He will not forgive us if we don't practice forgiveness toward others (see the scripture under this week's Blueprint).

Is it possible to forgive even when someone doesn't ask you to? What if the person doesn't acknowledge his or her sin against you? Is it still possible to forgive the offender? Yes, it is. It only takes two— you and God. God is the only one who can heal your hurt and help you forgive. Forgiveness is so much more than a gift you extend to others; it is a gift God first extends to you. Because of that gift, you can pay the healing benefits forward. It is like what John said in 1 John 4:19: "We love because God first loved us." Love and forgiveness are two of the gifts that just keep on giving! It is to your benefit to forgive. Without forgiveness, wounds can never heal.

We encourage you to remember that forgiveness takes two—you and God. Your ability to forgive is not based on the other person. As you forgive, you can also embrace forgiveness from others and from God.

God's Blueprint: *Putting God's Word into Your Relationship*

As you read the following scripture out loud, think about the very real consequences of not forgiving others.

MATTHEW 6:14–15

FOR IF YOU FORGIVE OTHER PEOPLE WHEN THEY SIN AGAINST YOU, YOUR HEAVENLY FATHER WILL ALSO FORGIVE YOU. BUT IF YOU DO NOT FORGIVE OTHERS THEIR SINS, YOUR FATHER WILL NOT FORGIVE YOUR SINS.

As you talk together about the questions below, think about the serious responsibility you have to forgive.

1. What are the benefits of forgiving past hurts, habits, or hang-ups?

2. Under what circumstances does God say He will not forgive you?
3. Why is it so difficult to forgive those who have harmed you but have never asked for forgiveness?
4. Share together a time when your loved one showed forgiveness toward you.

Home Improvement: *Start Where You Are and Grow*

1. What are some reasons that you should be a forgiver? Is there anything that needs to be forgiven in your relationship right now?
2. What are some reasons you are grateful for being forgiven by God and by those who love you? How does being forgiven make you feel?

Write about anything you are holding on to that you haven't yet forgiven, and then list some of the things you've done that require forgiveness.

HER THOUGHTS

_____

_____

_____

_____

_____

_____

_____

_____

_____

His Thoughts

_____

_____

_____

_____

_____

_____

_____

_____

_____

Team Building: *Grow Closer to Each Other as You Talk to God Together*

Read our prayers out loud, then using your own words, pray out loud together.

AL: My gracious heavenly Father, forgive me for my many sins as I forgive those who have sinned against me. Cleanse me from my past, my wounds, and the pain I have brought to those I love. Bless me with a healing spirit and a heart that always seeks forgiveness and relationship. I can pray this prayer because of the wounds of Christ on the cross, through Him, amen.

LISA: Dear God, You know my heart and You know what and who I need to forgive. Open my heart and speak to me. Penetrate my wounds with the balm of forgiveness. Please, Father, forgive my sins against You and others. As I make amends to You, help me to make amends to those I sin against. Through Jesus I pray, with the help of the Holy Spirit, amen.

A PERFECT SCENARIO

For all the years we've been together, we've heard Miss Kay and Phil (mostly Phil) discuss their sex life. Not in detail, mind you, but he just lets you know he enjoys his quiet time with Miss Kay. God created a beautiful thing between a husband and wife. It is not something we should be ashamed of or afraid of. It is the way God made us. Sometimes we get the cart before the horse, so to speak. Sex was designed by God to be a physical, emotional, and spiritual connection of intimacy. Commitment is meant to be sealed within the intimacy of the act. When we engage in sex without the bond of commitment and marriage, we can suffer from guilt, embarrassment, and fear of whether or not we can totally give ourselves to this other person. Outside of marriage and commitment, a void usually grows because we know something is lacking, and sometimes that void is directly linked to the lack of emotional and spiritual connection in the physical act of sex.

There are also many physical consequences that can result from sex outside of marriage. Disease and unwanted pregnancy can destroy lives and become generational curses. The very best way to have a guilt-free, disease-free, and embarrassment-free sex life is to live God's way. Waiting until we are husband and wife to share this special connection is the way God designed us. We did not adhere to God's plan and got the cart before the horse. We suffered a lot because of those bad decisions.

God sets up the perfect scenario for sexual intimacy, but He also makes provisions for when we don't conform to His idea of perfection. Don't let Satan keep you in guilt or embarrassment because of past sin, but aim for a committed relationship where sex is beautiful and unifying.

We encourage you to trust in God's perfect scenario and embrace forgiveness for any past mistakes. Start enjoying the great gifts He has designed for your relationship.

God's Blueprint: *Putting God's Word into Your Relationship*

As you read the following scripture out loud, notice the ways intimacy is portrayed.

GENESIS 2:22, 25

THEN THE LORD GOD MADE A WOMAN
FROM THE RIB HE HAD TAKEN OUT OF THE MAN,
AND HE BROUGHT HER TO THE MAN. . . .
THAT IS WHY A MAN LEAVES HIS FATHER AND MOTHER
AND IS UNITED TO HIS WIFE, AND THEY BECOME
ONE FLESH. ADAM AND HIS WIFE WERE BOTH NAKED,
AND THEY FELT NO SHAME.

Be honest and gentle as you discuss these important questions.

1. How was sex viewed in your home growing up? Was it discussed at all?
2. In what ways do you see sex as being more than just a physical act?
3. How do you deal with talking about the value of sex with each other and what do you do if there are problems in your sex life?
4. In what ways has your spouse made you feel valued through sex?

Home Improvement: *Start Where You Are and Grow*

1. What are some things that are important to your physical, emotional, and spiritual union with your mate?
2. What are some ways you want to grow in your intimacy with each other?

Record your honest answers to the two questions above.

HER THOUGHTS

_____

_____

_____

_____

_____

_____

_____

_____

His Thoughts

_____

_____

_____

_____

_____

_____

_____

_____

_____

Team Building: *Grow Closer to Each Other as You Talk to God Together*

Read our prayers together and out loud, then pray together about how you can grow intimacy in your marriage.

AL: Heavenly Father, thank You for building in us a love for commitment through marriage and for the wonderful gift of sex. Please help me strive to protect this gift and grow in my intimacy with Lisa. I pray this through Christ, amen.

LISA: Father, thank You for the institution of marriage. Thank You, God, that You provided us a way to enjoy our mates in our union. Forgive Al and me, Father, for having sex before marriage. Thank You for ridding us of our guilt, and help us to live and love and enjoy only each other in our marriage. Put on our hearts the job of telling others of Your perfect ways so that they too will be free of the hold that Satan places on us in our weakness. Through Your Perfect Sacrifice, Jesus, I pray, amen.

WEEK 23

GOD'S MIGHTY DEEDS

FIFTEEN YEARS INTO our marriage, we wondered if we were going to be able to make it another day. When we look back on those days now, we are amazed at what God did when we thought our marriage was finished. In the moment, the pain can be so intense that you aren't sure if you can make it another hour or even another minute. But God can take two willing vessels and totally transform what they think is broken beyond repair. As we look around today at our family, we are in awe of His great power. What if we had given up; what then? What would have happened to our kids? Would we have grandchildren or would our daughters have even had the courage to marry after their parents divorced? All these questions run through our thoughts today, but in the pain of the moment we never knew to ask them.

As you go through your life, there are times when you need to see the bigger picture—God's bigger picture. In order to see that picture, we must open up our attitudes to God's possibilities. He gave us the strength and endurance to stay together, to allow Him to change our hearts, and He gave us a new season. We will praise Him and tell others of His wonders for the rest of our days. And hopefully, we can encourage you to hold on through the pain and let God do what He does best. Try to have a positive attitude that new things are possible for you through Him. One of our greatest responsibilities is to offer people like you hope when all seems lost. There is no greater relief than the walk back from the edge of disaster to safety. We've made that walk by God's grace, and we can't keep quiet about it.

We encourage you to reflect on the positive, good things that have been done and seen throughout your relationship. Talk about the good things and build on them, and if you find yourself wanting to quit on your relationship, give God a chance to show you how wonderful it can be.

God's Blueprint: *Putting God's Word into Your Relationship*

As you read this short scripture out loud, think about things you thank God for.

PSALM 9:1

I WILL GIVE THANKS TO YOU, LORD, WITH ALL MY HEART;
I WILL TELL OF ALL YOUR WONDERFUL DEEDS.

Enjoy this discussion time as you talk about what God has done and your hopes for the future.

1. What are some things you've seen God do that amaze you?
2. What things have you overcome in your relationship because you were able to endure?
3. Name some of your hopes and dreams for the future of your relationship.

Home Improvement: *Start Where You Are and Grow*

1. Tell your mate about at least one of his or her positive attributes that reflect God.
2. What are some big-picture goals that you have for your relationship?
3. What do you need to give to God for those goals to be realized?

Talk together about your big-picture goals, then write down what you need to do in order for those goals to be accomplished.

HER THOUGHTS

_____

_____

_____

_____

_____

_____

_____

_____

_____

His Thoughts

_____

_____

_____

_____

_____

_____

_____

_____

Team Building: *Grow Closer to Each Other as You Talk to God Together*

Read our prayers together and out loud, then pray together about positively believing that God can do anything in your relationship.

AL: Lord, You are mighty in word and mighty in deeds. You created the universe and brought life from nothing, but You also care about what happens in my life and in my relationships. What a wonderful God You are! Help me to be ever aware of what You delivered me from and ever vigilant to never repeat the mistakes of my past. Help me be the man You created me to be, in Jesus name I pray, amen.

LISA: Father, when I think back on those days of uncertainty in my life and marriage, I am awed by Your commitment to transform my mind and heart and create in me a new being. I will never cease to praise You for Your unfailing love, grace, and forgiveness. Remind me each day to share the hope I have in You. Through Your son I pray, amen.

Compassion

WEEK 24

LEARNED TRAITS

THE ROBERTSON MEN, in general, are not very compassionate people. It's hard for them to show empathy or sympathy to others even if they have been in that person's shoes. This trait was passed on to them from our Granny and Pa, Phil's parents. But as the Robertson men have grown older, they have learned that in order for them to help others, there are times when compassion is needed. As fathers, they have learned this as well. It's still not easy and may not be their first response, but once they step back a minute and take a deep breath, they realize that kindness and compassion are needed. They recognize this default reaction as a weakness of character and will always struggle with their first instinct to blame someone else, because that is how strong generational imprinting can be. Even if kindness and compassion are not your first response, you too can learn to be more like Jesus.

Forgiveness has been another learned trait for the Robertson men. They don't hold grudges, it's just hard for them to forgive and trust. They tend to be leery. But again, as they have grown in their faith, they are now able to forgive and eventually to trust—where it's wise to trust.

If you share this or other learned and passed-down traits, continue to allow God to work on your heart. We don't want to just give in to things God doesn't desire by claiming, "Well, that's just how

I was raised!" Blaming our upbringing is an excuse to continue in ungodly ways.

Jesus was kind, compassionate, forgiving, and perfect in every area of His life. If we strive to be like Jesus, we must strive to be like Him in every way.

We encourage you to allow God to teach you and rewire your heart so you react and respond just like He would.

God's Blueprint: *Putting God's Word into Your Relationship*

As you read the scripture below, notice the motivation we are given to forgive.

EPHESIANS 4:32

BE KIND AND COMPASSIONATE TO ONE ANOTHER, FORGIVING EACH OTHER, JUST AS IN CHRIST GOD FORGAVE YOU.

Use this time to share memories and stories of your past that relate to how you are today.

1. What negative traits did you learn from your family of origin? What needs to be done in your life to redirect your heart and actions?
2. Can you relate to the struggle of being compassionate and kind?
3. Why is it impossible to have a healthy relationship without the ability to forgive?

Home Improvement: *Start Where You Are and Grow*

1. What excuses do you use to not be kind, compassionate, and forgiving?
2. What can you do to grow in these areas?
3. What positive traits do you see in your mate that encourage growth in you?

Write about both the negative and positive traits that you learned from your family, then write what traits you want to pass on to your next generation.

HER THOUGHTS

_____

_____

_____

_____

_____

_____

_____

_____

_____

HIS THOUGHTS

_____

_____

_____

_____

_____

_____

_____

_____

_____

Team Building: *Grow Closer to Each Other as You Talk to God Together*

Read our prayers below out loud; then pray together about unlearning negative traits and growing in compassion.

AL: Father, I am so grateful to You for giving me a mate who is good at things I am not so good at. She completes me and helps us be stronger as a couple. I am growing in the area of compassion and empathy, and I pray You help me break the cycle that has been my legacy in this area. Thank You for Jesus who, by His grace, makes up for all our weaknesses. In Him I pray, amen.

LISA: Father, as I go about my life, striving to be in the image of Jesus, help me to be kind, compassionate, and forgiving. These three qualities are the heart of Jesus, and I want to be just like Him. I know I will fail at times, but Father, forgive me and teach me to take the time to think about what Jesus would do and how He would react to the situations I find myself in. In Jesus' name, amen.

TONGUE WRANGLER

Y OU MAY FIND this week's devotional title funny, but it's actually a biblical term, well . . . sort of. We are told to keep a tight rein on our tongue, so what else would you call that? In James 3, we read about the tongue being compared to a bit in the mouth of a horse. James makes the point that a bit is a small thing, like a tongue, but it controls where the whole, big horse will go. He goes on to describe the tongue as a small spark that can set a whole forest ablaze. You get the idea. Though the tongue is a very small thing physically, it affects every aspect of our lives. If we don't wrangle our tongue to get it under control, the results can be devastating, especially in our relationships.

When our kids were small, they loved the movie *Bambi*. It forced us to explain death and nature and why we hunted, but they eventually understood. We loved the part of the movie when Thumper's mama hears him talking about someone. The words she says spoke volumes to us and then to our daughters. She asks Thumper to say, "If you can't say something good, don't say nothing at all." Our daughters still quote that movie as a reason they should watch what they say about other people. We must be careful not to frame our words of destruction as "constructive criticism." Though we want to be honest, we must "speak the truth in love," as another Bible writer said in Ephesians 4:15, always being aware that our tongues have great power to hurt as well as to heal. James says our religion is worthless if we can't wrangle our tongues.

We encourage you to think before you speak and to remember that yours may be the only religion some folks see.

God's Blueprint: *Putting God's Word into Your Relationship*

As you read this scripture together, you may think of some people who don't keep a tight rein on their tongues. You can learn from them what not to do, but try to look at yourself too.

JAMES 1:26

THOSE WHO CONSIDER THEMSELVES RELIGIOUS AND YET DO NOT KEEP A TIGHT REIN ON THEIR TONGUES DECEIVE THEMSELVES, AND THEIR RELIGION IS WORTHLESS.

This discussion may be difficult, so remember to control your tongue and "speak the truth in love."

1. Do you struggle with not wrangling your tongue?
2. Why is our religion worthless if we don't control our tongues?
3. How do you balance honesty and constructive criticism with being too harsh—especially in your relationship with your loved one?
4. Tell your loved one about a particular time he or she was truthful yet kind while addressing a difficult topic.

Home Improvement: *Start Where You Are and Grow*

1. What do you need to work on regarding how you use your tongue?
2. How can you be honest and speak the truth in love and yet not abuse others with your words?
3. What are some positive things you need to say more to those you love?

This is another one of those times when you need to focus on what you need to do as you write about the questions above.

HER THOUGHTS

_____

_____

_____

_____

_____

_____

_____

_____

_____

His Thoughts

_____

_____

_____

_____

_____

_____

_____

_____

_____

Team Building: *Grow Closer to Each Other as You Talk to God Together*

Read our prayers out loud; then pray together about controlling your words.

AL: Lord, I have so many good opportunities to say things that help people, build them up, and encourage them. Help me to maximize those opportunities and minimize the harsh things I say to others, especially to those closest to me. Forgive me when I hurt with words and tear others down. I know it's wrong, and I know it can have terrible consequences. Bless me with words full of grace and salt—words that preserve and encourage. Thank You for Christ and His words of healing and hope. Through Him I pray, amen.

LISA: God, you know I am sometimes guilty of speaking before thinking. I often want to crawl under a rock after I've spoken unkind words. Please help me to speak in a way that shows that I can control my tongue. Forgive me, Lord, when I hurt others with the words from my wild tongue. In Jesus' name, amen.

Grace

GRACE TONIC

W**E HAVE A** large family, and we don't always agree with each other. We all have different personalities, different likes, and we come from a lot of different backgrounds. It is one of the reasons we believe our television show, *Duck Dynasty*, has been so successful. People have related to the fact that large families don't always agree but that ultimately you pull together instead of fracturing apart. When the cameras aren't rolling, we strive to keep one another on target and to hold one another accountable, and we accomplish this by being loving and forgiving and by extending grace to one another. While we want each person in our family to be himself or herself, we also want all of us to behave like men and women created in the image of God—people who are willing to be molded by God's holiness and character and integrity.

We do not want any one of us to fall short of the glory of God. Something terrible happens when people move away from God and family, and it's called *bitterness*. Bitterness takes root in the spiritual heart of someone and is difficult to dig out. The longer it holds and grows, the more devastating and difficult it is to remove. Because we've seen so many families and relationships destroyed by bitterness, we are vigilant to make sure it doesn't happen to us. We must have an attitude of gratitude for each person in our family, celebrate our differences, and constantly check our attitudes toward each other. We have control over what makes us bitter, and grace is the special tonic that cures the sour nature of bitterness.

We encourage you to root out any potential bitterness *now*, before it burrows deep in your heart, and to live in such a way that grace stands guard over your heart.

God's Blueprint: *Putting God's Word into Your Relationship*

As you read the verse below out loud, ask yourselves if you currently have a "bitter root" in your relationship that will grow up to cause trouble if you don't uproot it now.

HEBREWS 12:14–15

MAKE EVERY EFFORT TO LIVE IN PEACE
WITH EVERYONE AND TO BE HOLY;
WITHOUT HOLINESS NO ONE WILL SEE THE LORD.
SEE TO IT THAT NO ONE FALLS SHORT
OF THE GRACE OF GOD AND THAT
NO BITTER ROOT GROWS UP TO
CAUSE TROUBLE AND DEFILE MANY.

Use the questions below to talk about how these principles apply to your relationship—not only how they apply to you as individuals.

1. Why do you think the writer in Hebrews links *peace* with *holiness*?
2. How does bitterness grow and defile?
3. Why does grace become the tonic for bitter feelings?
4. Share with your loved one how he or she has shown you grace when bitterness could have been an option.

Home Improvement: *Start Where You Are and Grow*

1. How can you better connect to God's holiness?
2. What can you do to be more graceful toward those around you?
3. Are there any bitter seeds planted in your spirit that you need to let go of before they take root?
4. Have you ever asked someone who loves you to point them out? How did that go?

Before you write this week, ask God to search your heart and see if there is any "offensive" thing in you (read Psalm 139:23–24). Write about what God reveals to you.

HER THOUGHTS

_____

_____

_____

_____

_____

_____

_____

_____

_____

_____

_____

_____

_____

_____

_____

_____

_____

Team Building: *Grow Closer to Each Other as You Talk to God Together*

Read our prayers together and out loud, then pray together about discovering and uprooting any bitterness in your hearts.

AL: Heavenly Father, I am so honored to be a receiver of Your grace. You rescued me from my own sinfulness, and because You are perfect and holy, I actually share in that perfection and holiness—amazing! I have no ability to be holy without You; please forgive me when I try to be. Remove any bitter seeds in my heart and replace them with the saving grace of Your holiness. Help me to be like You and treat others the way I want to be treated. Thank You for Christ; it is through His sacrifice that I come in confidence, amen.

LISA: Father, please help me to allow You to rid me of all bitterness. I ask that You cleanse my heart, mind, and soul of the things that cause me to choose bitterness. Please forgive me and make my soul new and clean and free from Satan's hold through my bitter thoughts. Because of Jesus and through Him I pray, amen.

WEEK 27

A SIMPLE CHARGE

IN EPHESIANS CHAPTER 5, the apostle Paul gives a great picture of what it looks like to be a follower of God. He closes the chapter by using marriage as an illustration of how the relationship between God and us works. This approach shows us how closely our human relationships are intertwined with our heavenly relationships. From the Garden of Eden until now, God has used our love for others as a picture of what it is like for Him to respect and love us, and for us to love and respect Him. Submission and sacrifice are the foundational elements of our relationship with God, and they are also the foundation of our love for man and woman as husband and wife.

Paul closes chapter 5 with a simple and poignant charge: Husbands love your wives, and wives respect your husbands. Sounds simple enough, right? We all know that simple words don't always translate into simple actions. But we have discovered an easy way to make this directive work in our marriage. Al works on being more respectable, while Lisa works on being more lovable! We decided we wanted each other to have an easy time of living up to his or her end of the bargain. It's amazing how this perspective has changed our lives and our relationship.

The Word of God is the best place to start, and we found two passages to help us: Proverbs 31 (for a woman's lovability) and Job 31 (for a man's respectability).

We encourage you to read these texts with a heart and mind open to how they can make you both grow in love and respect and make each other's jobs easier. Over the next two weeks, we will dive into these passages a little more deeply.

God's Blueprint: *Putting God's Word into Your Relationship*

Read the scripture below together and out loud, and notice the two very specific commands for your relationship with your loved one.

EPHESIANS 5:33

EACH ONE OF YOU ALSO MUST LOVE HIS WIFE AS HE LOVES HIMSELF, AND THE WIFE MUST RESPECT HER HUSBAND.

Be open to God's teaching and try not to be defensive as you discuss being lovable and respectable.

1. Why do you think marriage is used as an illustration by Paul when talking about a Christian's relationship with God?
2. What roles do sacrifice and submission play in the divine-human relationship? What roles do they play in human relationships? In marriage?

3. Why does it seem so difficult to look at ourselves when we see a directive like Ephesians 5:33, versus looking at the shortcomings of our mate, which seem to jump right out at us?

4. Tell your loved one about a time he or she was lovable or respectable.

Home Improvement: *Start Where You Are and Grow*

1. What kind of plan will you put in place to help you work on being more lovable?
2. What kind of plan will you put in place to help you be more respectable?

Again, focus on yourself as you write about how you can be more respectable and more lovable.

HER THOUGHTS

_____

_____

_____

_____

_____

_____

_____

_____

His Thoughts

_____

_____

_____

_____

_____

_____

_____

_____

_____

Team Building: *Grow Closer to Each Other as You Talk to God Together*

Read our prayers together and out loud, then pray about each of your simple charges from Paul—to love and respect.

AL: Heavenly Father, I thank You for the relationship I have with You and that You taught me how to love by first loving me. We respect You and fear You because You are worthy of all worship, praise, and awe. Please instill in me a heart of love for my mate, and help me look more like Your Son, Jesus, who sacrificed Himself that I might live for eternity. Help me to turn away from my own selfish desires and to show more love and respect. I humbly ask for this in Christ's name, amen.

LISA: Father, I ask that You help me to love my mate like You love me. I pray, Father, that I will emulate Your example of unconditional love even when I don't think my mate is worthy of respect. I pray that, together, we can become more lovable and respectable in each other's eyes, but more important in Your eyes. Please forgive me when I fail. In Jesus' name, amen.

More Lovable

LISA: When you read this section, it would help if you'd open your Bible to Proverbs 31 and read the portions we talk about here.

When I've wanted to find ways to be more lovable, I've always started with verse 10, but I find it interesting that when you read verses 1–9, you see that King Lemuel's mother is the one who taught him these things. She was trying to equip her son to choose a godly wife and to be a respectable man. Lovability is introduced in this chapter as something that should be taught to sons and daughters and passed on as a matter of high importance. While Scripture challenges my husband to be more lovable, I want to set the pace by being everything God has called me to be as a believing wife, mother, and grandmother.

In verses 10–31, I learn that as a wife, I need to infuse confidence in my husband, and that happens best when I am trustworthy and honest. I need to bring him good, not harm, and strive to be a wife in good standing with those who know me. I must strengthen our home, which means I am the main caretaker of the home, and I must manage our family and see that everyone is fed, homework is done, baths are taken, and prayers are said. It is my job to exude compassion and help those who are less fortunate and to allow my children to see this compassion. I must have a sense of humor, because let's face it, some days it's either laugh or cry! Laugh more and let your kids know that God is in control. Finally, I must fear the Lord. My beauty is fading on the outside daily, but as I grow in the Lord, my inner beauty and strength shine through to my outward appearance.

I encourage you to show others that a godly life is the eternal beauty secret and that your man will find it easy to love you more and more.

God's Blueprint: *Putting God's Word into Your Relationship*

As you read the scripture below out loud, notice whether it's written specifically to men or women or to both.

ROMANS 12:9–10

LOVE MUST BE SINCERE. HATE WHAT IS EVIL; CLING TO WHAT IS GOOD. BE DEVOTED TO ONE ANOTHER IN LOVE. HONOR ONE ANOTHER ABOVE YOURSELVES.

Let the woman in the relationship do most of the talking in questions 1–3.

1. Why is it important to live and teach the principles expressed in the portrait of the lovable woman in Proverbs 31?

2. What are the difficulties in consistently living out this love that we have been challenged to exhibit?

3. Why does the woman in a home seem to be the key to whether that home exhibits love or doesn't?

4. Guys, tell your loved one about a time she was especially lovable.

Home Improvement: *Start Where You Are and Grow*

1. Women, what are some things you can do to exhibit the example of the woman described in Proverbs 31?
2. What will you have to change about yourself to be more like her?
3. Men, what are some things you can do to help your mate achieve the lovability challenge she has received?

Women, as you consider the questions above, write about what God revealed to you about what you need to change. Men, write about how you can make it easy and rewarding for your soul mate to make the changes God has convicted her to make.

HER THOUGHTS

_____

_____

_____

_____

_____

_____

_____

_____

HIS THOUGHTS

_____

_____

_____

_____

_____

_____

_____

_____

_____

Team Building: *Grow Closer to Each Other as You Talk to God Together*

Read our prayers together and out loud, then pray together. Men, you might pray about how you can better appreciate the blessing your loved one is. Women, you might pray about areas you want to grow in to be more lovable.

AL: Father, I have been so blessed by the gift of a woman who has grown through all our years together. She has become more lovable every year we have been together, and we both know that You are the reason why. I praise You for her being reborn in a way that has brought love into our family, respect into our marriage, and praise and respect for me as one of your godly servants. Continue to bless her growth and my love for her, as we serve You and teach our children and grandchildren to follow Your ways. I pray this through Jesus Christ, amen.

LISA: God, I can't imagine my life without You in it. You have blessed me every day of my life. I pray, Father, that I can be a lovable woman, mother, wife, grandmother, and friend. I pray that my actions toward others will reflect my heart toward You. I want to be just as You described in Proverbs 31. I want to be a blessing to my Lord, my husband, my family, and my community. Please create in me a pure heart to be the woman You created me to be. Through Jesus, amen.

More Respectable

AL: Job 31 is an interesting place to go to see what a man needs to do to live more respectably. Job was in a bad place when he spoke these words. He was defending his character and integrity, as he was being attacked by his friends because of some tough times he was going through. I find his defense of who he was and how he lived to be a tremendous challenge for me as I strive to be more respectable.

Job begins his challenge by bringing up one of the most difficult things for most men to do: protect your eyes and mind from looking and lusting after other women. He goes on by offering honesty as the next logical step, which is how you overcome the first challenge. Hiding in deceit and shadows only fuels sin in a man's heart and life. Next, Job challenges me to protect my faithfulness to Lisa by warning me not to behave inappropriately toward other women, avoiding any hint or possibility that I may belie my integrity. He then reminds me that if I want others to treat me with respect, I must treat them with respect—never putting others down because they are in a different position in life than I am. He challenges me to be generous and not to view career or wealth in this life as more important than what is most important—my relationship with God and my relationship with my family. He lastly encourages me not to seek vengeance upon those who have wronged me and to let God handle those things for me.

I want my mate to respect me because I am a respectable man. What would an honest defense of my life look like?

I encourage you to take an honest look at your respectability and figure out what an honest defense of your life would look like.

God's Blueprint: *Putting God's Word into your Relationship*

Men, as you read this scripture out loud, you might think about why respect is important to you and whether you are a respectable man.

PROVERBS 31:23

HER HUSBAND IS RESPECTED AT THE CITY GATE, WHERE HE TAKES HIS SEAT AMONG THE ELDERS OF THE LAND.

Both of you answer the first two questions.

1. Outside of your relationship with your spouse, whom do you respect? What about these people has led to this respect?
2. Why was Job so adamant about defending the way he lived his life? Why was respect so important to him at this stage in his life?
3. Men, why is it important to you that you be respected and respectable?
4. Women, share at least one thing about your man that you respect.

Home Improvement: *Start Where You Are and Grow*

1. Men, what are some ways you plan to work on being more respectable? What will you need to change for that to happen?
2. Women, what can you do to help your mate gain respect in his daily life? How does your being more lovable help him be more respectable?

It's a little tough to think about whether you are respectable and lovable. Use the space below to write about where you need to grow and what you'll do to make that growth happen.

HER THOUGHTS

_____

_____

_____

_____

_____

_____

_____

_____

_____

His Thoughts

_____

_____

_____

_____

_____

_____

_____

_____

_____

Team Building: *Grow Closer to Each Other as You Talk to God Together*

Read our prayers below out loud, then pray together. Men, you might pray about how you might be respectable—especially as you think about how Job's defense of his integrity applies to you. Women, you might pray about how you can show respect to your man through your words and actions.

AL: Heavenly Father, I am challenged by these words from Job to be a better man. I fall short in several of these areas, and I know that my respectability falls with it. Forgive me for not being all I should be. I humbly ask for strength and wisdom as I offer up my eyes, my heart, my body, and my soul to You for refinement and refreshing. I want the love of my life to find it easy to respect me in her ongoing quest to love and cherish me. I ask for these things in the name of Jesus Christ, our Lord, amen.

LISA: Jesus Christ, we are all sinners You died for. I fall short in so many ways. I pray, Father, that You touch my mate and give him the strength to be the man You made him to be and not what the world expects him to be. We want to be different. This world is not our home. Teach me to be in this world but not of this world. I pray blessings on my husband right now, God. Change him, make him new, make him Your man. Only through His name, Jesus, amen.

DON'T MISS YOUR MOMENT

NOW THAT WE have the luxury of over thirty years together, we can look back over the course of our lives and see key moments that shaped where we are today. Some moments were career-related, some were key for the development of our children, while others were crucial for us to work through issues as a couple. Looking back at key moments is great, but anticipating them and looking ahead to make the right decisions is far more important.

A great biblical example of a guy who made the most of his opportunities was Joseph, whom you can read about in Genesis 37–50. He had a tremendous gift of prophetic dreams from God, and his father recognized this and favored him. His older brothers were extremely jealous and sold him into slavery, telling their father he had been killed. This lie broke the old man's heart and started Joseph as a teenager on an odyssey he could never have been prepared for. Even though he continued to make good decision after good decision, it seemed on the surface he wasn't being rewarded for those decisions. For thirteen long years, he labored for others and was even thrown into prison.

Joseph did the right thing again and again and finally got an opportunity to use his prophetic gift to interpret the dreams of the pharaoh of Egypt. He was elevated to a position equal to a prime minister, and at thirty years old was second only to Pharaoh. God had been looking out for him all that time, even though it didn't appear so. We believe that the key moment of Joseph's life came in Genesis 45:1–15 when he faced his brothers in the palace of Pharaoh. He had the power to avenge himself, but instead he recognized God's will for him, forgave them, and embraced them.

Joseph's life is a great example of how powerful forgiveness is and how it keeps bitterness from creeping into our hearts.

We encourage you to practice forgiveness every single day in your relationship, and we encourage you to make the most of every moment, especially when given the opportunity to overlook an offense.

God's Blueprint: *Putting God's Word into Your Relationship*

Read the scripture below out loud, and think about how it relates to Joseph and forgiveness and to you.

EPHESIANS 5:15–17

BE VERY CAREFUL, THEN, HOW YOU LIVE—NOT AS UNWISE BUT AS WISE, MAKING THE MOST OF EVERY OPPORTUNITY, BECAUSE THE DAYS ARE EVIL. THEREFORE DO NOT BE FOOLISH, BUT UNDERSTAND WHAT THE LORD'S WILL IS.

Think together about the key moments in your life and the role forgiveness played in them.

1. What are some key moments in your relationship that helped shape where you are today? Did forgiveness play a role in any of those moments?
2. Why was the time of deciding whether or not to forgive his brothers such an important moment in Joseph's life? How do you think it affected his psyche and his life within his own family?
3. Why is daily forgiveness and daily striving to understand God's will so important for you as a couple trying to maintain a close relationship?
4. Share with your loved one a key moment when he or she forgave you and how much that meant to you.

Home Improvement: *Start Where You Are and Grow*

1. Looking back, what are some big moments when you did the right thing at a key time? What are some moments that you blew it and did the wrong thing?

2. What can you do to be better prepared for key moments in the future? How can you better understand what God's will is for you and your relationship?

Think about when in your life you decided to forgive and when you didn't. Write about the differences those decisions have made in your life. Think about whether there is anything you need to forgive your loved one for right now. What will you do about that?

HER THOUGHTS

_____

_____

_____

_____

_____

_____

_____

_____

HIS THOUGHTS

_____
_____
_____
_____
_____
_____
_____
_____
_____

Team Building: *Grow Closer to Each Other as You Talk to God Together*

Read our prayers together and out loud, then share in prayer together.

AL: Father, thank You for guiding me through all the turbulence of my life and using me to accomplish things for Your glory. I have missed many opportunities to show how great You are, but because of Your grace, I have managed to get a lot of things right—especially the most important things. Forgive me for my failures and inspire me to always choose forgiveness and mercy when faced with vengeance. I know You will always make things right, and I trust in Your eternal power of righteousness and judgment. I have this confidence because of Christ, my Savior, and I pray through His name, amen.

LISA: Lord, thank You for the examples You give us in the Bible. Sometimes I tend to think my problems are unique to me and that no one else struggles or has struggled with them before. Father, help me to use the example of Joseph and choose forgiveness over bitterness. I have had many opportunities to choose bitterness over forgiveness. I wish, Father, I had always chosen forgiveness, but You are aware of my failures. Please, Lord, help me live a life of forgiveness and love, as You lived Your life here on earth. Please forgive me when I fail. Holy Spirit, use my failures as a reminder for me to make good, godly decisions each day. In Jesus' holy name, amen.

TRUTH OR LIES?

DID YOU EVER play the "two truths and a lie" game? Do you remember the premise of the game? Tell two things that are true and one that is false, and let others figure out which one is the lie. This is supposed to be an icebreaker game to get to know people better. We have used it in camp settings, and it helps the participants to learn other people's histories. Unfortunately, through the years, we have seen this pastime as not just a game but as a lifestyle choice for many people. What happens when lies are a part of the way you live?

Maybe your game is two lies and a truth or maybe three lies and no truth. The book of Proverbs talks a lot about lying lips and truthful lips. In the past, our relationship was plagued with untruths. We now know that things in our past made us feel as if we couldn't be truthful with each other. We experienced the ultimate lie in a marriage—an affair. What we found was that an affair will either cure you of being untruthful or it will kill your relationship for good. It is one of the most destructive weapons Satan uses to destroy relationships and families. It usually starts with one lie that leads to others until it is a full-blown way of life.

Thanks to God, He rescued us and put us on a truth-filled path. One of our favorite verses compares honesty to a kiss on the lips.

This concept speaks directly to our honesty with each other just as it relates to our intimacy with each other. No one likes kissing lying lips.

We encourage you to keep your lips truthful and your heart honest. If you do this, you will gain the most intense intimacy you can imagine.

God's Blueprint: *Putting God's Word into Your Relationship*

Read this scripture out loud and think about what honesty and kisses have in common.

PROVERBS 24:26

AN HONEST ANSWER IS LIKE A KISS ON THE LIPS.

These questions will help you get to the heart of why dishonesty is sometimes our default. Think through them carefully and answer honestly.

1. Why is it sometimes so hard to be honest about our lives, both past and present?
2. Do you find it hard to receive honesty, especially when it hurts to hear the truth? How does that factor into fostering dishonesty?
3. How does dishonesty affect intimacy between a couple?
4. Tell your loved one about a time you appreciated his or her honesty, even though it may have been difficult to say and to hear.

Home Improvement: *Start Where You Are and Grow*

1. What specific ways can you grow in honesty?
2. How can you help your mate grow in honesty?
3. How can you be a better receiver of your mate's honesty?
4. What changes do you need to make to help your relationship be one of total honesty and intimacy?

Write about things you may need to be honest about and how you can create an atmosphere that makes your loved one feel safe enough to tell the truth.

Her Thoughts

_____

_____

_____

_____

_____

_____

_____

_____

His Thoughts

_____

_____

_____

_____

_____

_____

_____

_____

_____

Team Building: *Grow Closer to Each Other as You Talk to God Together*

Read our prayers together and out loud; then pray together about being honest with your mate and putting away any lies.

AL: Father, thank You for being the wellspring of truth and the exact opposite of dishonesty, and for receiving my dishonesty with grace and mercy. You tell us that it is impossible for You to lie, and I believe that and strive to be more like You in everything I think, everything I act upon, and every way I live. Help me to be honest with my soul mate and to receive her honesty with grace, mercy, and love. We long for the day when dishonesty will be impossible for us. We live with that great hope because of Jesus, our Savior, amen.

LISA: God, my Redeemer, You are my truth and my salvation. I've had problems with lying lips, Lord, but You have shown me the path of honesty. Thank You, Father! Please help me to always keep a truthful answer on my lips. I love to be kissed by my man, and I know he likes kissing honest lips. Teach me to tell the truth even when a lie seems easier. In Jesus' name, amen.

BORN TO BE CHOSEN

ONE OF THE tasks we assign to premarital couples when we counsel them is to write a letter to their respective in-laws thanking them for having and raising their future mates. We've found this to be a great way to deepen a very important relationship and keep the in-laws from becoming out-laws! It also tells one's mate that they were born and raised to be chosen for this relationship, which is a huge encouragement and a lovely thought.

We have witnessed Willie and Korie's love as they've made multiple decisions to adopt and embrace children from newborns to teenagers. They believe that the children they've taken in and loved were born to be chosen to be part of the Robertson family and to be impacted for all eternity by our family's faith in the gospel of Christ. Of course their children who were born to them share that same blessing. This same love is applied to the decision to commit oneself in marriage to the person who was born to complete and fulfill you—if you believe, as we do, that marriage is for the entire length of our lives here on earth.

We have had the double blessing of choosing each other for life, in good times and bad, in sickness and in health, through thick and thin, and also being chosen by Christ through our obedience by faith to His gospel story. What a hope as we continue on our journey!

We encourage you to express to your mate and to God your appreciation for to your mate and to God for being chosen for a great relationship.

God's Blueprint: *Putting God's Word into Your Relationship*

Read the scripture below out loud, and notice what God has chosen and predestined you for.

EPHESIANS 1:3–5

PRAISE BE TO THE GOD AND FATHER OF OUR LORD JESUS CHRIST, WHO HAS BLESSED US IN THE HEAVENLY REALMS WITH EVERY SPIRITUAL BLESSING IN CHRIST. FOR HE CHOSE US IN HIM BEFORE THE CREATION OF THE WORLD TO BE HOLY AND BLAMELESS IN HIS SIGHT. IN LOVE HE PREDESTINED US FOR ADOPTION TO SONSHIP THROUGH JESUS CHRIST.

As you talk together, think about how much you appreciate that God chose your loved one just for you.

1. Why do you think God chose your loved one for you?
2. How does the realization of being chosen by God—through your faith in Him—help you better appreciate your mate and your family?
3. How does having a lifetime commitment help your relationship stay strong?
4. Share with your mate some of the reasons God chose him or her for you.

Home Improvement: *Start Where You Are and Grow*

1. What are some things you appreciate about your soul mate? (Feel free to share those.)
2. What can you do to ensure a lifelong commitment to the growth of your relationship?

Write down some of the things you've talked about during this devotional.

HER THOUGHTS

_____

_____

_____

_____

_____

_____

_____

_____

HIS THOUGHTS

_____

_____

_____

_____

_____

_____

_____

_____

_____

Team Building: *Grow Closer to Each Other as You Talk to God Together*

Read our prayers together and out loud, then pray together from your hearts.

AL: Father, it is an honor to be able to call You "Father." I am so grateful that You chose me as a son because of my faith in You. I feel special because I know I am a co-heir with Christ to the entire universe, all because of my being Your son. I thank You even more for removing my sins and allowing me to be blameless because of the sacrifice of Christ. Thank You for my soul mate, and thank You that her parents birthed her, raised her, and gave her to me to spend the rest of my life with. I pray that my legacy will make You proud of me, Your son. I am able to approach You only because of my brother Jesus' sacrifice of Himself on the cross, amen.

LISA: Dear God, I want to say thank You for allowing me to be your child. I had a great earthly father, but You, Lord, will give me life eternally. I want to make You proud that You chose me to be Your child. I will live my days telling others of Your great love, forgiveness, grace, and about Your adoption of me through my spiritual death. I died to myself, but Father, I live completely in You, forever! Thank You, Jesus, for making all this possible by sacrificing Yourself for me. Through Your name, I pray to our Father, amen.

Affection

THE POWER OF TOUCH

WHEN OUR OLDEST daughter, Anna, was born, she was eleven weeks premature and weighed only one pound and fifteen ounces. We were very young but old enough to be scared to death and doubtful she would survive. After a heart surgery and three and a half months in the hospital, we brought her home on Father's Day in 1986, reasonably healthy and weighing four whole pounds! She has now blessed us with three granddaughters, and we thank God for blessing us with her.

For those three and a half months in the hospital, we went to visit and spend time with her at every opportunity because we knew instinctively that our presence was important for her survival. We couldn't hold her for the first couple of months, so we would just stroke her legs and arms and rub her head. Affectionate touch was so important for her and for us, and it is something we have never forgotten.

When you read in Matthew, Mark, Luke, and John about all the people Jesus healed throughout His short time on earth, it is amazing how many sick people He touched. He is the Son of God, so He didn't have to touch them to heal them, but He did. He even touched some who had diseases that caused them to be untouched by anyone. We believe Jesus was giving us an example for how we should be with one another.

Affection may not come naturally to you. In our relationship, Lisa is naturally affectionate, Al not so much—probably because he's a Robertson. But he has grown in that area.

We encourage you to daily give affirming and affectionate touch to your mate and to others you love.

God's Blueprint: *Putting God's Word into Your Relationship*

Read this verse out loud, and notice that John is talking about actually touching Jesus when He was on earth. Think about the implications of this verse for your relationship.

1 JOHN 1:1

THAT WHICH WAS FROM THE BEGINNING, WHICH WE HAVE HEARD, WHICH WE HAVE SEEN WITH OUR EYES, WHICH WE HAVE LOOKED AT AND OUR HANDS HAVE TOUCHED— THIS WE PROCLAIM CONCERNING THE WORD OF LIFE.

Understanding each other's past and present feelings about touch will help you as you increase the touch and affirmation in your relationship.

1. How natural is affection and touch for each of you? Is it something you experienced growing up?

2. Why is touch important in a relationship? Talk together about the level of importance touch holds for you.

3. Why do you have to be careful when it comes to touch outside of your relationship and family?

4. Tell your spouse about a special time when his or her touch meant a lot to you.

Home Improvement: *Start Where You Are and Grow*

1. What opportunities do you currently have to affectionately touch your mate every day?
2. How can you add more touches with your mate? How can you grow in affectionate touches to others in your family?
3. If either of you has any hang-ups from your past that make touch uncomfortable for you, talk about that together.

Write about specific times and ways you can give touch to your loved one, and about any relationships you need to remove touch from.

HER THOUGHTS

_____

_____

_____

_____

_____

_____

_____

_____

His Thoughts

_____

_____

_____

_____

_____

_____

_____

_____

_____

Team Building: *Grow Closer to Each Other as You Talk to God Together*

Read our prayers together and out loud, then pray together about how you can use touch appropriate to your relationship (married or not married) to show sincere affection.

AL: Father, You have touched my life in such a powerful way, and I praise You for loving me enough to save me from my sin. I long for the day I will literally be in Your presence and express my adoration face to face. Thank You for showing me how important affection is, even though I didn't experience it a lot when I was growing up. Help me to grow in affection for my mate and my family and guard me from any inappropriate affection toward anyone outside my marriage. Thank You for Jesus and His power to touch and save, amen.

LISA: Lord, You made me to be a touchy-feely person. I am grateful for that. I love to touch, hug, kiss, and love on my family. I pray, Father, that I can be more in love with You every day and have conversations with You like I do with my family. I long for the day when I sit in Your presence and can be touched by You. You are the great physician and healer. Thank You for healing me and setting me free by the blood of Jesus. Through Him I pray, amen.

Unity

UNITED WE STAND

ONE OF THE early struggles in our marriage was figuring out how two people raised so differently could get along. Al is the oldest in his family, and Lisa is the youngest in hers, and just that difference alone caused a lot of arguments. We loved each other but viewed things from different perspectives. We didn't have the maturity to appreciate our differences then. We thought we had to change each other to become exactly like ourselves, and this led to a lot of trouble. Mistakenly, we were striving for uniformity instead of unity, and it took us a long time to understand this.

Through the years, we have grown so much in our unity that now we actually celebrate and embrace our differences and realize we are more complete *because* of our differences. The only way we achieved this unity was to have a common goal: getting ourselves and our family to heaven. Every new goal flowed out of that one, and while we could compromise on some things to maintain unity, we would never compromise our relationship with God.

Of course, we are imperfect, so there will always be struggles to maintain unity and make the right decisions, but we have discovered that with Christ at the center of our lives, we now live much more peacefully than in our early days together. We strive to always consider each other above ourselves, and we are amazed at how much better our marriage is because of this principle.

We encourage you to embrace your differences and live with the blessing of unity in your relationship.

God's Blueprint: *Putting God's Word into Your Relationship*

Read this scripture out loud, and think about what it means to "make every effort" to keep unity in your relationship.

EPHESIANS 4:1–3

I URGE YOU TO LIVE A LIFE WORTHY OF THE CALLING
YOU HAVE RECEIVED. BE COMPLETELY HUMBLE AND
GENTLE; BE PATIENT, BEARING WITH ONE ANOTHER
IN LOVE. MAKE EVERY EFFORT TO KEEP THE UNITY
OF THE SPIRIT THROUGH THE BOND OF PEACE.

Talk openly about barriers to unity in your relationship and what you can do to "keep the unity."

1. Talk about the differences of your upbringings. How does your birth order affect how you relate to each other?
2. Why does the scripture above link humility, gentleness, patience, and love to unity?

3. Talk about how peaceful or unpeaceful your relationship is. What can you both do to increase the peace?

4. Share with each other a time that you felt especially close to and loved by your mate.

Home Improvement: *Start Where You Are and Grow*

1. What are you doing that causes disunity in your relationship and home?
2. What effort do you need to make to maintain unity in your relationship? What can you change about your attitude or actions?

Write about the things you need to do differently to bring about and maintain unity.

HER THOUGHTS

_____

_____

_____

_____

_____

_____

_____

_____

His Thoughts

_____

_____

_____

_____

_____

_____

_____

_____

Team Building: *Grow Closer to Each Other as You Talk to God Together*

Read our prayers together and out loud, then pray together about building unity in your relationship.

AL: Lord, I am eternally grateful for the unity we share because of the sacrifice of Jesus. Because He died for me, I can now enjoy a relationship, even though I am totally unworthy. You have taught me what it means to live in peace, and I want to foster that peace more and more in my relationships. Help me to make every effort to live in unity with my mate, my family, my forever family, and even my enemies. Through Christ, I make this appeal, amen.

LISA: Jesus, I am so grateful for Your Spirit that lives in me. I know I've made a lot of mistakes along the way, but Your Spirit has never left me. You have taught me to be "one in spirit" with those in my life and to be "one in my marriage." Al and I don't always agree, but our disagreements don't divide us anymore. They strengthen us. Thank You, Father, for sending Jesus to save me and give me an advocate in heaven. Jesus is my only hope for eternal life. I look forward to living in unity rather than uniformity. Because of the cross, amen.

Hospitality

A Place of Refuge

WHAT DO YOU remember about growing up in your home? Was your home a place of refuge or chaos? Did your family do a lot of entertaining, or were outsiders rarely invited in? We were raised differently, and our homes reflected that difference. Al grew up in a home that had lots and lots of people in and out every day. Miss Kay always cooked extra because they were always entertaining and reaching out to people. The cleanliness of her home was not a big deal to her. The condition of the heart of people was what mattered most. When Al went to bed at night, he never knew who or how many he would find asleep on the couch or floor when he awoke the next morning. Their doors were never locked, and he would usually find a pair of wet clothes left by a baptized new brother or sister who had decided to give his or her life to Christ during the night. Even though his home was loud and chaotic, he loved being there. Lisa's home was always clean and quiet but rarely had people in it. There were family issues that led to arguing and fighting, and this made home a place she and her sister rarely wanted to be. To her, home felt like a prison, not a sanctuary.

When we married, we wanted our home to be a place of refuge. We wanted our children to feel love and be content. We wanted people to come into our home and feel that love and contentment.

We wanted to serve others in the way Alan's parents did when he was growing up and as Lisa witnessed during the time they dated. We wanted a home that was safe but friendly, and where people enjoyed visiting. We wanted a home that was hospitable.

To practice hospitality and have people feel comfortable in your home, you and your family must feel comfortable as well. Strife-filled people rarely want to practice hospitality because they don't feel it. Peace-filled homes allow their occupants to invite and be-friend others in order to bring them into the home to break bread to-gether or to talk about the Bread of Life.

We encourage you to have a home filled with love, contentment, peace, and hospitality. It's never too late to change the dynamic of your home. Hospitality will change the folks who live within your home, and God will receive glory.

God's Blueprint: *Putting God's Word into Your Relationship*

Read this scripture aloud, and think about your family of origin as you do. Also think about how you want your home to change or remain the same.

ROMANS 12:13
SHARE WITH THE LORD'S PEOPLE WHO ARE
IN NEED. PRACTICE HOSPITALITY.

Talk openly with each other about the kind of home you want to have.

1. What are your memories of the home you grew up in?
2. Is hospitality something you are used to, or is this a whole new concept?
3. What is your home like today? Do you think your family sees it as a refuge and a place they want to share with others?
4. Share with each other about a time and a home where you felt very welcome and loved.

Home Improvement: *Start Where You Are and Grow*

1. What can you do to ensure more peace in your home?
2. What do you need to do to start having people into your home?
3. How can you be more hospitable?

Write about the hospitality or lack thereof in the home you grew up in. Then write your plans for how your home can be different or similar.

HER THOUGHTS

_____

_____

_____

_____

_____

_____

_____

_____

HIS THOUGHTS

_____

_____

_____

_____

_____

_____

_____

_____

_____

Team Building: *Grow Closer to Each Other as You Talk to God Together*

Read our prayers together and out loud, then pray together about what you want hospitality to look like in your home.

AL: Father, I am very grateful for the home I grew up in. It wasn't perfect, but it was loving—especially after Mom and Dad became Christians. I am so thankful for their hearts to share what You did in their lives. Help us to be vigilant to keep our home friendly and inviting to others. Forgive us for being selfish with our great blessings by failing to share what we have and show hospitality. We pray this through Christ our Lord, amen.

LISA: Father, I am grateful we live in a home of peace and love. I am grateful we can help others find Jesus in our home. Help us to always appreciate the home You have blessed us with. I'm grateful for every place that we have been able to live in and make a home. You have always given us a place of peace and refuge, no matter how big or how small our home was. You are our provider and sustainer. Keep us humble and grateful. In His Name, amen.

TRUST AND OBEY

ONE OF THE greatest challenges in our marriage has been maintaining trust in each other. A lot of poor decisions before and after we were married resulted in mistrust. Without divine help we would not still be together. One lesson we have learned from our mistakes is that we must prove ourselves worthy of trust if we want to be trusted. In other words, until you do trustworthy things, your partner won't know whether or not you can be trusted!

A biblical story that has helped us work on trusting God and trusting each other is the story of Naaman in 2 Kings 5. We encourage you to read that story together. Naaman was a powerful man and a military commander, but he had leprosy, which would have made him socially untouchable in his culture. He attempted to buy healing in Israel from a prophet of God named Samuel but was angry and disappointed when his money was refused and he was simply told to go dip himself in the dirty Jordan River seven times to be healed. A wise servant convinced him to get over himself, and Naaman finally humbled himself and trusted in the simplicity of God's command through Samuel, and he was, indeed, healed.

We can relate to this story because we realize that we are imperfect and can become prideful. When we are tested to do simple things that bring health to our relationship, we sometimes fail to trust and act. Thankfully, there are people in our lives who help us remain humble, and we are also honest enough with each other to work on maintaining trust and faithfulness.

We encourage you to be open and honest with each other and to be patient if your spouse needs time to rebuild trust in you.

God's Blueprint: *Putting God's Word into Your Relationship*

Read this scripture out loud, and think about what specific "trust" the writer is talking about here.

1 CORINTHIANS 4:2
NOW IT IS REQUIRED THAT THOSE WHO HAVE
BEEN GIVEN A TRUST MUST PROVE FAITHFUL.

Trust is a crucial part of any close relationship. Take your time talking through these questions.

1. Do you think it is fair that God says He will test your trust and faith in Him? Why or why not?
2. Why should you expect that your trust in others be tested?
3. How have you had to rebuild trust in any of your relationships, either their trust in you or your trust in someone else?
4. In what ways can you relate to Naaman?
5. Tell your loved one about a time that you were able to fully trust in him or her and why that meant so much to you.

Home Improvement: *Start Where You Are and Grow*

1. What can you do to help your mate trust you more?
2. What are some things you need your mate to do to help you trust him or her more?
3. What do you need to grow in spiritually to help prove your faithfulness to God?

Take time to write about your trust of your mate and his or her trust in you—and how you can help bring about needed changes.

HER THOUGHTS

_____

_____

_____

_____

_____

_____

_____

_____

_____

HIS THOUGHTS

_____

_____

_____

_____

_____

_____

_____

_____

_____

Team Building: *Grow Closer to Each Other as You Talk to God Together*

Read our prayers together and out loud; then pray together, openly and kindly.

AL: Heavenly Father, I praise You because You are always faithful and because You never fail me in our relationship. I wish I could say the same about me, but we both know I can't. Forgive me for failing You again and again, and help me to strive to be more like You. I thank You for Your grace, and I pray for growth in becoming trustworthy to You and to my soul mate. Through Jesus, I humbly offer this prayer, amen.

LISA: Lord, I pray I can be a trustworthy person. I have not always been this way, and I have let others down. Thank You for the ability You give us to rebuild trust in each other. I pray that trust, truth, and honesty reign in my life until the day You return. I pray I can help instill these principals in the people You send to me, whether family or friend. Help me to be an example to others and to be trustworthy always. Through Jesus I pray, amen.

CULTURE WARRIORS

WE HAVE CERTAINLY seen a lot of changes in our culture during our lifetimes, and like generations before us, we tend to lament the general decline of goodness and morality. The cycle of civilizations declining into the abyss of moral decay is well chronicled throughout human history, including the thousands of years recorded in the Bible. For our family, the key question is, "How are we going to survive and thrive in our culture?"

One of the saddest family tragedies recorded in the Bible is the story of Lot and his family in Genesis 18–19. We encourage you to read that story together. Lot came from a strong family of faith and leadership with his Uncle Abraham and Aunt Sarah, but when he moved to the big city, things digressed for him and his family. The culture was so toxic and evil in the twin cities of Sodom and Gomorrah that God decided to destroy them by natural disaster. When given the opportunity to flee the oncoming destruction, Lot's daughters' fiancés and his own wife didn't trust Lot enough to follow him and his daughters out of the city. What's even more disturbing is that Lot was all too willing to offer up his daughters to an angry mob before the city was ultimately destroyed. Quite honestly, Lot failed his family miserably and left a legacy of cultural compromise rather than being a warrior for what was right in his culture.

It is so important to engage the culture around us with the strength of our Almighty Father and the safety of a unified relationship and family. We can't sit it out and we can't go it alone, or we will fail and the coming generations will suffer. We must fight to protect the values and morals God expects of us and not be brought down by the world around us.

We encourage you to assess your surroundings, make a game plan to best engage the culture for God, and humbly hold each other and your family accountable—making sure you aren't giving in to the world around you but are protecting the Truth God gave us.

God's Blueprint: *Putting God's Word into Your Relationship*

Read this scripture aloud, and think about things of "the world" that you love and how you need to refocus your love.

1 JOHN 2:15–17

DO NOT LOVE THE WORLD OR ANYTHING IN THE WORLD. IF ANYONE LOVES THE WORLD, LOVE FOR THE FATHER IS NOT IN THEM. FOR EVERYTHING IN THE WORLD—THE LUST OF THE FLESH, THE LUST OF THE EYES, AND THE PRIDE OF LIFE—COMES NOT FROM THE FATHER BUT FROM THE WORLD. THE WORLD AND ITS DESIRES PASS AWAY, BUT WHOEVER DOES THE WILL OF GOD LIVES FOREVER.

It's easy to get swallowed up in our culture; think about yourself and about your surroundings and how they affect you.

1. What is glaringly bad about your immediate surroundings?
2. What are some things that used to bother you but now don't? Why the change?
3. Why does John say you can't love the world and God? Why does it have to be one or the other?
4. Tell your loved one about a time when he or she chose to stand up against something bad in your culture and how that made you feel.

Home Improvement: *Start Where You Are and Grow*

1. What are some of your fears about the current culture and how it relates to your family?
2. What things should you be doing to engage the culture for good?
3. What habits do you need to change to be in a better position to impact your culture for good?

Write about what's good and bad about the culture you live in and how you can stand up against what's wrong and protect what God says is right.

HER THOUGHTS

_____

_____

_____

_____

_____

_____

_____

_____

_____

His Thoughts

_____

_____

_____

_____

_____

_____

_____

_____

_____

Team Building: *Grow Closer to Each Other as You Talk to God Together*

Read our prayers out loud and together, then thoughtfully pray about your culture and how you can impact it for good.

AL: Lord, I am worried about the way our culture is headed, and I want our family not only to survive but to thrive in the midst of it all. Help me to lead and not follow and also to be a proper example to my own family. I pray for my grandchildren and for my future progeny to stand strong in the face of what is sure to be difficult times. I pray for Your return to take us all to heaven before things get too bad. I love You deeply and pray for a revival of and a turning to You in our world. I approach You humbly by the grace and blood of my Lord, Jesus, amen.

LISA: Father, I am concerned about what is happening in our country and in this world. The ideals that I hold dear and the morals I was taught are being trampled upon. I cry out to You, Lord, to help me stand firm! Father, help me to put on my armor and fight for the Truth that I find in Your Word. I pray for our future generations that they too will stand firm against Satan and his attacks on Christianity. Come soon, Lord, we are ready! Because of Your Son, Jesus, amen.

ANGER MANAGEMENT

WE ARE BLESSED that neither of us has a bad temper, but that doesn't mean we have not struggled with anger issues throughout our relationship. To struggle with anger is to be human, because of all the emotions, anger has one of the highest potentials for destructive behavior and damage to relationships. The struggles of so many relationships begin with anger and then launch into other damaging habits. While we tend to blame anger, the real problem is what we do with anger and how we respond in it.

If you researched anger in the Bible, it might surprise you to learn that God is angry a lot, which lets us know that anger itself is not sinful. But without righteousness, anger will lead to many sins. James says in James 1:19–20 that we should "be slow to become angry, because human anger does not produce the righteousness that God desires." If we are honest with ourselves, we know that teaching is true. For whatever reason, some people seem to have a harder time with anger, especially related to temper. If this is a problem for one or both in a marriage, then the relationship is constantly in potential danger.

Stuffing anger down is toxic and not healthy, but going nuclear and scorching the relationships around you is not healthy either. Only God can truly change your anger to kindness, and He does this through the soothing work of His Holy Spirit, whom He sends to His followers to guide and counsel.

We encourage you to look openly and honestly at how you are when you get angry and to allow God to work in you to make sure your relationship is not hurting from anger.

God's Blueprint: *Putting God's Word into Your Relationship*

As you read the following scripture out loud, notice how we can be angry without sinning; also take note of what God tells us to "get rid of."

EPHESIANS 4:26, 31

"IN YOUR ANGER DO NOT SIN": DO NOT LET
THE SUN GO DOWN WHILE YOU ARE STILL ANGRY. . . .
GET RID OF ALL BITTERNESS, RAGE AND ANGER,
BRAWLING AND SLANDER, ALONG WITH
EVERY FORM OF MALICE.

Notice how your friends can affect the effect of anger in your life.

PROVERBS 22:24–25

DO NOT MAKE FRIENDS WITH A HOT-TEMPERED PERSON,
DO NOT ASSOCIATE WITH ONE EASILY ANGERED, OR YOU
MAY LEARN THEIR WAYS AND GET YOURSELF ENSNARED.

Be honest about your own anger as you discuss these questions together.

1. How often do you get angry enough to make outbursts or to need to be calmed down?

2. Why is it so important not to hang on to or stuff our anger, as mentioned in the Ephesians passage above?

3. The writer in Proverbs implies that angry behavior can be catching. Do you find this to be true? How can that happen and what are the usual results?

4. Share with your loved one a time you saw him or her rein in anger and how that made you feel.

Home Improvement: *Start Where You Are and Grow*

1. What things do you find yourself being consistently angry about?
2. What are some ways you can change how you respond, even if you're angry?
3. What spiritual things can you do to help yourself be less angry, especially in your relationships?

Getting a handle on your anger is vital. Be honest with yourself as you consider the questions above and write your thoughts below.

HER THOUGHTS

_____

_____

_____

_____

_____

_____

_____

_____

_____

His Thoughts

_____

_____

_____

_____

_____

_____

_____

_____

_____

Team Building: *Grow Closer to Each Other as You Talk to God Together*

Read our prayers together and out loud, then pray together about how you can better manage anger personally and in your relationship.

AL: Father, I am grateful that I do not anger easily, and I never want to take the Holy Spirit who lives inside me for granted. Please help me to stay open to the gentle leading of the Spirit and to allow Him to bear His fruit in my spirit. Forgive me when I fall short of this and say or do things in anger that are sinful. I never want to live in such a way that You would be angry with me. In humility, I ask these things through Jesus, with the help of Your Spirit, amen.

LISA: Thank You, God, that I am a "controlled" person most of the time. There are times when I do get angry and respond sinfully. Please forgive me, Father. Please help me to be angered by what angers You but to follow Your example to not sin in my anger. Please give me the spirit of righteousness without the spirit of self-righteousness. I am blessed that You gave me a mate who is not easily angered. Help us to never go to sleep angry at each other. In Your Son's name, I pray, amen.

EMPOWERING WORDS

HAVE YOU EVER stopped to think just how powerful words are? When we were children, we used to say, "Sticks and stones can break my bones, but words can never hurt me." Someone came up with those words to try to protect children, but in reality, words really do hurt, especially when we are young and developing. Another thing we used to believe is that we could take back words we said to or about others. Once you get a little older, you realize you can never take back words once they are said. We can't unhear what we hear.

In our marriage, we have certainly been guilty of saying hurtful things to others and have been on the receiving end of each other's words as well. Early in our relationship, we said a lot of harsh things to each other, and we regret every one of them. Thankfully, we changed those bad habits and discovered something else wonderful about words: they have the power to heal and build up!

What you say and, even more important, how you say it can have a huge, positive impact on your mate, your family, and anybody you come in contact with. Tone, body language, and demeanor are all crucial elements in saying things that build up rather than tear down. The New Testament writers consistently warn about speaking when angry because they know how difficult it is to keep from hurting those around us when we are in this state of mind. If we disagree about something or we're upset about something, we have learned to wait before we discuss solutions. There is wisdom in waiting until everyone is calmer and thinking clearly about a response.

Other things we work to take out of our communication are sarcasm and coarse joking about each other. We both have a sense of humor and actually believe it is crucial to enjoying life, but never at the expense of hurting others, especially the ones we love the most.

We encourage you to take a really good look at your communication habits, especially how you talk to each other. Your relationship will only get better as your words get better.

God's Blueprint: *Putting God's Word into Your Relationship*

Read this scripture aloud, and notice the writer's strong and beautiful words about how we are to speak to one another. Take to heart what you need to apply to yourself.

COLOSSIANS 3:8; 4:6

BUT NOW YOU MUST ALSO RID YOURSELVES OF ALL SUCH THINGS AS THESE: ANGER, RAGE, MALICE, SLANDER, AND FILTHY LANGUAGE FROM YOUR LIPS. . . . LET YOUR CONVERSATION BE ALWAYS FULL OF GRACE, SEASONED WITH SALT, SO THAT YOU MAY KNOW HOW TO ANSWER EVERYONE.

Share honestly as you go through the questions below.

1. How have you been adversely affected by others' words to or about you?
2. What dangers are associated with speaking while angry, upset, or disappointed?
3. What do you think the writer of the Colossians passage above means by "full of grace, seasoned with salt"?
4. Share with your loved one a time you saw his or her words full of grace or seasoned with salt.

Home Improvement: *Start Where You Are and Grow*

1. What bad communication habits do you need to get rid of?
2. What good communications skills do you want to begin or increase?
3. How can I improve the communication between my mate and myself?

Write about the things you need to get rid of in your life and the things you need to add.

Her Thoughts

_____

_____

_____

_____

_____

_____

_____

_____

HIS THOUGHTS

_____

_____

_____

_____

_____

_____

_____

_____

_____

Team Building: *Grow Closer to Each Other as You Talk to God Together*

As you do each week, read our prayers together and out loud, then use your own words and thoughts to pray together.

AL: Father, I am sorry for the times when I have flippantly used words to demean or wound. Please forgive me for not being wiser with my words. I want the words I use to build up and make a difference to people, especially those whom I love the most. Help me, Lord, to think before I speak and to show restraint with my words. I humbly ask this in Jesus' name, amen.

LISA: Jesus, I am an "open mouth, insert foot" kind of girl sometimes. I don't want to be. I want to be a person of encouragement—speaking love and empowering people around me. Help me to rid myself of the things that tear others down. Allow my words to make friends and not break relationships. In Him, Your Son, I pray, amen.

UNEQUALED FORGIVENESS

A S A COUPLE, when you survive infidelity in your relationship like we did, it changes your perspective on so many things. Guilt, shame, honesty, trust, and forgiveness take on a whole new meaning in your everyday thinking. Stories in the Bible are not just stories about someone else; they become your story as well. The story in John 8 about the woman caught in adultery is one we relate to now in a completely different way. It shows us the unequivocal forgiveness that Jesus offers to us. A woman was brought to Jesus by the teachers of the law and Pharisees because they caught her in the act of adultery. By law she could have been stoned to death for her sin, but Jesus made the case for grace and appealed to the onlookers with stones in their hands to look at themselves before taking out justice on this woman.

What we love most about the story is that Jesus didn't bring out a pad that listed all her sins and tell her about each one. You know there were more; no one gets to the point of adultery without first having lost their way. We love that Jesus also saw the sins of the ones who were there to stone her. Sometimes we forget we are all sinners. Sins are not graded by God. One is enough to separate us. But Jesus, being the gentle, forgiving, and forthright man he was, said, "Where are they? Has no one condemned you?" Of course when the woman opened her eyes and looked up, they were gone. Imagine the thoughts going through her head. Then imagine how her heart felt after these words: "Then neither do I condemn you. Go now and leave your life of sin."

Ah, what sweet relief. He knew her life consisted of other hurts, sins, and actions that had gotten her to that point. Forgiveness! There is nothing like it when it comes to relief and burdens being lifted and also nothing like it to motivate you to live differently.

We encourage you to seek forgiveness from our heavenly Father and from those you have harmed; then extend that same relief to someone who may have hurt you.

God's Blueprint: *Putting God's Word into Your Relationship*

As you read the passage below out loud, think about what touches you most about this scene.

JOHN 8:3,7, 9–11

THE TEACHERS OF THE LAW AND THE PHARISEES BROUGHT IN A WOMAN CAUGHT IN ADULTERY. THEY MADE HER STAND BEFORE THE GROUP. . . . WHEN THEY KEPT ON QUESTIONING HIM, HE STRAIGHTENED UP AND SAID TO THEM, "LET ANY ONE OF YOU WHO IS WITHOUT SIN BE THE FIRST TO THROW A STONE AT HER." AT THIS, THOSE WHO HEARD BEGAN TO GO

AWAY ONE AT A TIME, THE OLDER ONES FIRST, UNTIL
ONLY JESUS WAS LEFT, WITH THE WOMAN STILL STANDING
THERE. JESUS STRAIGHTENED UP AND ASKED HER,
"WOMAN, WHERE ARE THEY? HAS NO ONE CONDEMNED YOU?"
"NO ONE, SIR," SHE SAID.
"THEN NEITHER DO I CONDEMN YOU," JESUS DECLARED.
"GO NOW AND LEAVE YOUR LIFE OF SIN."

*As you answer the questions below, open your hearts to remember the
sweetness of forgiveness you have felt.*

1. Why would they bring only the woman caught in adultery and
   not the man she was with?
2. What are some of the times in your life when you felt the sweetness of forgiveness from Jesus? From others?
3. How does this passage give you hope that God can and will
   forgive our sins?
4. Share with your loved one about a time that his or her forgiveness helped you heal.

Home Improvement: *Start Where You Are and Grow*

1. How can you offer forgiveness to each other on a daily basis and not allow Satan to build a wall of resentment in you? How can you receive forgiveness for some of your past hurts?

2. Are you ready to offer forgiveness to your spouse, family member, friend, and others who have hurt you? Are you ready to accept forgiveness for your part in the hurts of others? If you are, start now. There is no better time than the present. If you aren't, then continue to pray for God to help you with your forgiveness. Prayers offered in humbleness and brokenness give God the tools to soften those wounds.

Write about where you are in your journey toward forgiveness and what you think your next step needs to be.

HER THOUGHTS

_____

_____

_____

_____

_____

_____

_____

_____

Team Building: *Grow Closer to Each Other as You Talk to God Together*

Read our prayers together and out loud, then pray together about forgiveness in your lives.

AL: Heavenly Father, I am humbled by Your willingness to continue to forgive my sin. I am eternally grateful for the sacrifice of Your Son and I pray I can be like Him when others sin against me. I humbly accept Your love and pray that I will pay it forward to others. Your grace uplifts me and sustains me, and I never want to take it for granted. Because of Christ I offer this prayer, amen.

LISA: Father, we all need forgiveness. Thank You for allowing me to be forgiven and also for the ability to forgive. Sometimes I tend to judge others with a different scale than I use to judge my own sins. Help me, Father, to see that the sins in my life and the sins of others are the same to You. Your forgiveness, Your sacrifice, Your blood on the cross is sufficient to remove all the sin, hurt, damage, and open wounds in my heart and soul. Help me, Lord, to look to You for the healing of my heart and soul. Through Your Son, our Savior, we pray, amen.

A POWERFUL CONFESSION

LISA: When honesty has not been a part of your life, you tend to make excuses for your failures. True honesty makes it easier to confess your wrongs. I was not an honest person for most of my life. At thirty-five, I found myself not knowing who I was. I was never honest about my life. I was a woman caught in adultery who wanted to blame everyone around me for my being there. I was molested as a young girl, I was abandoned by my first love, I had an abortion as a teenager, I cheated, I stole, and I lied to everyone, including myself. All of those things were very good reasons to falter, but I could no longer use them as excuses. I had to face reality and face myself. I had to travel a hard road, but God Almighty gave me the strength, the forever family, and the husband and his forgiveness to accomplish what I once thought was impossible. I looked at the mess I was and decided I didn't like what I saw. What would I do?

I was married to the preacher of our church. Most would say I couldn't be honest with everyone because I would lose their respect: confess it to God and a few close friends and move on. What did I do? I marched myself right to the front of the church and spilled it all. You see, I knew that if I didn't get it all out in the open, then I would forget the sin I saw in my life and never change fully. I needed the eyes of the church on me. I was not respectable! I needed to show my church family that I needed them to help me change. More than all that, I wanted Jesus to know I was serious. I wanted my husband to know I was repentant. I wanted the accountability of my elders and church leaders. I wanted honest confession! I wanted prayers so I could be healed. I wanted my sins covered by the blood of Jesus. I was done with deceit. I would not cover up my iniquity any longer. I wanted the guilt of my sin to be forgiven. What did I get? That and whole lot more! But none of it would have happened if I had not been honest and confessed my sins to my brothers and sisters in Christ.

I encourage you to express honest confession to each other, to God, and to your church family. It will heal your soul.

God's Blueprint: *Putting God's Word into Your Relationship*

As you read these scriptures out loud, notice the power of forgiveness and think about how it affects your life.

JAMES 5:16

THEREFORE CONFESS YOUR SINS TO EACH OTHER AND PRAY FOR EACH OTHER SO THAT YOU MAY BE HEALED. THE PRAYER OF A RIGHTEOUS PERSON IS POWERFUL AND EFFECTIVE.

PSALM 32:1–2, 5

BLESSED IS THE ONE WHOSE TRANSGRESSIONS ARE
FORGIVEN, WHOSE SINS ARE COVERED. BLESSED IS THE ONE
WHOSE SIN THE LORD DOES NOT COUNT AGAINST THEM AND
IN WHOSE SPIRIT IS NO DECEIT. THEN I ACKNOWLEDGED
MY SIN TO YOU AND DID NOT COVER UP MY INIQUITY.
I SAID, "I WILL CONFESS MY TRANSGRESSIONS TO THE
LORD." AND YOU FORGAVE THE GUILT OF MY SIN.

As you talk about these questions together, try to lay down your fear and be honest with each other.

1. How is true confession healing to the soul?
2. What are the barriers to being as open as Lisa was about her life?
3. How healthy is it to keep things from your mate about past or present sins?
4. Tell your loved one what his or her honesty means to you.

Home Improvement: *Start Where You Are and Grow*

1. What are some things you need to be open about that may be preventing healing in your life and in your relationship together?

2. How can you as a couple help each other have honest confession?

3. How will you help your spouse change once he or she has made their confession?

Take this time to honestly write about your need for forgiveness and how you can help your mate.

HER THOUGHTS

_____

_____

_____

_____

_____

_____

_____

_____

_____

His Thoughts

_____

_____

_____

_____

_____

_____

_____

_____

_____

Team Building: *Grow Closer to Each Other as You Talk to God Together*

Read our prayers together and out loud, then pray together about honesty in your relationship.

AL: Father, I openly confess I am a sinful man who daily needs Your grace to survive. I am so thankful for the healing that takes place when I am honest with You and with those around me. Thank You for loving me in spite of my flaws and for rewarding my honesty with love and salvation. I pray that I will be like You and will be a good receiver of honesty and dispenser of grace and mercy to those who confess to me. I pray this in confidence because of Christ, amen.

LISA: Lord, I am in awe of the healing power of confession. I know it is a very private matter, but I know that You give us a forever family to help us when we confess. Teach me, Lord, to be honest with who I am. Allow me to see others as You see them, with the blood of Jesus on their heads cleansing their sins. Show me the people I need to encourage to confess the sins that so easily entangle them. Thank You, Jesus, for the blood that washes me white as snow. In Your name I pray, amen.

Parenting

INSTILLING DISCIPLINE

WHO LOVES DISCIPLINE? Who loves to discipline? Who even likes to see discipline happen? We can tell you that as grandparents, we do not like to watch it happen to our grandchildren. We may not like it, but we know it is necessary and have a lot of respect for our own children for disciplining our grandchildren. We are multigenerational when it comes to discipline, as we believe that the discipline that has been handed down is the reason our families remain intact and our children are respectful as they mature.

All the Robertson brothers have practiced strong discipline, and the world has peeked in through our television show to see a functioning family that has respect for others. Jep and Jessica have the youngest children in our family, and we wondered how well they would do with all our success. Their four children have some of the sweetest hearts and best attitudes of the whole bunch! We believe a lot of that has to do with the discipline their parents have instilled in them from an early age. They've learned that certain actions bring certain consequences. Their little hearts are so sweet to others, including their siblings. Do they fight? Well, of course they do. They're brother and sisters, and sibling rivalry has gone on since the beginning of time, but they love one another and it shows. They want what's best for one another and they know that, ultimately, God will be pleased with their ways. They also love their cousins and their friends and know they have to forgive the wrongs of others. How do we teach this? It starts at home.

We don't like discipline in our own adult lives, but we know it's necessary for us to grow and be respectful. God disciplines us so we can grow in understanding, faith, obedience, and love. Isn't that what we want for our children as well? How can we discipline others if we are undisciplined ourselves?

We encourage you to embrace discipline for your own life and your lives as a couple, and to work on instilling that discipline into the lives of your children and future generations.

God's Blueprint: *Putting God's Word into Your Relationship*

As you read the scriptures below aloud, think about how discipline "produces a harvest of righteousness and peace."

PROVERBS 13:24

WHOEVER SPARES THE ROD HATES THEIR CHILDREN, BUT THE ONE WHO LOVES THEIR CHILDREN IS CAREFUL TO DISCIPLINE THEM.

HEBREWS 12:11

NO DISCIPLINE SEEMS PLEASANT AT THE TIME, BUT PAINFUL. LATER ON, HOWEVER, IT PRODUCES A HARVEST OF RIGHTEOUSNESS AND PEACE FOR THOSE WHO HAVE BEEN TRAINED BY IT.

If the discipline you received as a child was harmful instead of helpful, talk about that too.

1. How has discipline helped you to be who you are today? Were you disciplined fairly and consistently as a child?
2. How does God's discipline prepare you for passing along discipline to future generations?
3. How has discipline prepared you for your relationship together?

Home Improvement: *Start Where You Are and Grow*

1. What are some areas in your personal and spiritual life in which you need to have more discipline?
2. What are some ways God seems to be trying to teach you something now through discipline?
3. How can you help each other to use godly principles when you discipline your children?

Use this time to write about how discipline has shaped your life—even if it was not wise or helpful discipline—and how you intend to emulate that discipline or how you intend to do things differently with your children.

HER THOUGHTS

_____

_____

_____

_____

_____

_____

_____

_____

His Thoughts

_____

_____

_____

_____

_____

_____

_____

_____

_____

Team Building: *Grow Closer to Each Other as You Talk to God Together*

Read our prayers together and out loud, then pray together about God's discipline in Your lives and your discipline in the lives of your children.

AL: Father, I am grateful for the discipline You have given me throughout my life, even though it wasn't pleasant at the time. I know that because of Your love for me, You have trained me to be a better person. I thank You for Your guidance and the ability You have given me to do the same for my children and now my grandchildren. Help me to be consistent and fair in my discipline and to continue to receive Your correction until that great day of the resurrection. I ask this prayer through Christ, amen.

LISA: God, You are my Father. You train me daily to do what is right. You teach me to obey the rules You have set before me. Help me, Father, to teach and train my children and grandchildren to obey your commands as I train them for service in Your kingdom. Help each of us to discipline as You would: with love and truth. In His name, I pray, amen.

WEEK 43

IT'S NOT ABOUT ME

AFTER SPENDING SO many years in full-time ministry, it has been an interesting transition for us to be back working and living outside of the church. While pastoring a church, it's too easy to think of yourself more highly than you ought to because people constantly sing your praises. Of course that praise is usually balanced by those who criticize you, which can make you feel worse about yourself than you probably should. A good friend of ours built the pulpit that Al preached behind for twelve years, and on the side that only the preacher sees, he engraved, "It's Not about Me!" What a great friend to remind a man of God that a good sermon or a bad sermon is not the preacher's to possess but God's to deliver through him.

The same sentiment needs to be present in our relationships as well. In our life and our experiences with others, we find that selfishness is at the root of most relationship troubles. When we find ourselves mired in the thinking of "I and me" instead of "us and we," a crisis is almost always looming. The standard of the Christian faith is selflessness, which is fully displayed in the example of Jesus Christ. Jesus was and is God, yet He submitted Himself on our behalf to become a human being and then allowed Himself to be put to death. When we started viewing each other through the eyes of Christ, we saw things completely differently. Our marriage changed for the better when we began to think of each other instead of ourselves.

We encourage you to take on the challenge of putting selfishness to death and to have a relationship based on humble selflessness.

God's Blueprint: *Putting God's Word into Your Relationship*

As you read the scripture below, consider how "looking to the interests of others" would look in your relationship.

PHILIPPIANS 2:3–5

DO NOTHING OUT OF SELFISH AMBITION OR VAIN
CONCEIT. RATHER, IN HUMILITY VALUE OTHERS ABOVE
YOURSELVES, NOT LOOKING TO YOUR OWN INTERESTS
BUT EACH OF YOU TO THE INTERESTS OF THE OTHERS.
IN YOUR RELATIONSHIPS WITH ONE ANOTHER,
HAVE THE SAME MINDSET AS CHRIST JESUS.

As you talk together about these questions, think more about how you need to be less selfish rather than how your spouse does.

1. Why is the concept of selflessness so difficult to live out consistently?
2. In what ways should Christians have a huge advantage over nonbelievers in their relationships?

3. The Philippians writer mentions selfish ambition or vain conceit. What role does ambition, vanity, or conceit play in the problem of selfishness?
4. Tell your mate about a time that his or her selflessness was noticed and appreciated.

Home Improvement: *Start Where You Are and Grow*

1. Ask your loved one to tell you honestly about your level of self-lessness.
2. In what ways do you tend to respond selfishly?
3. What things can you begin to do to become more selfless, especially in your relationships?

Use this time to search your heart for areas of selfishness and write about what you can do differently to think more about your mate's interests than your own.

HER THOUGHTS

_____

_____

_____

_____

_____

_____

_____

_____

HIS THOUGHTS

_____

_____

_____

_____

_____

_____

_____

_____

_____

Team Building: *Grow Closer to Each Other as You Talk to God Together*

Read our prayers together and aloud, then pray together about how you can replace selfishness with selflessness in your lives.

AL: Lord, I am so happy You have chiseled me down from the selfish person I once was to a man who is a little more like Your Son, Jesus. I realize I still have a long way to go and that I need to keep working on my attitude, my vanity, and my pride. Forgive me when I mess up, and keep working in me to help me be the man You called me to be. I want to always think of You first, then my mate, then my family before I think of myself. Help me in this life struggle, in Jesus' name, amen.

LISA: Father, it is so easy for me to get caught up in myself. We are taught at a young age to say "mine." My toys, my movies, my phone, my computer. As adults, we move on to say "It's my life." Please, Father, help me move past the *me* and think in terms of our lives, our family, our things, and our God. Help us to understand that everything belongs to You. In Jesus' name, amen.

A BEAUTIFUL CHILD

S MANY KNOW, we have a very special child in our family. Mia is one of a kind. She was born with a cleft palate and cleft lip. Jase and Missy found this out on an ultrasound while Missy was pregnant. It was difficult for them because they had no idea how mild or severe a case it would be. They started researching doctors right away. When Mia was born, it was a little terrifying for Jase and Missy. Since then, we have seen worse cases, but when it's your child or a child you love, it's tough. Mia has had six surgeries so far; number six was the worst and, we hope, the worst she will ever have to endure. Each time, we have seen Jase and Missy persevere through the difficulties. We can't imagine being in their shoes, but we walk alongside them trying to help carry their burden and supporting them with love and encouragement.

In Galatians 2:13–14, the apostle Paul told the church at Galatia, "As you know, it was because of an illness that I first preached the Gospel to you, and even though my illness was a trial to you, you did not treat me with contempt or scorn. Instead, you welcomed me as if I were an angel of God, as if I were Christ Jesus himself." Paul used whatever was going on with him physically to make a huge spiritual impact. We feel this is exactly what has happened with Jase, Missy, and Mia.

Mia has told her story to thousands of people. We know now why

Mia was given to Jase and Missy. They had the knowledge to teach her about Jesus. They had the strength to persevere so that when the will of God is done, they will receive what is promised. All this was done out of love for their little girl. They wanted her to receive the treatment she needed to live a healthy life, but she has received so much more than that! Mia will continue to share her story and God's story, and as she grows in her faith and perseveres in her life, she will become mature and complete. She will not lack anything, and others will hear about God.

We encourage you to persevere in your trials so that when you have done the will of God, you will receive what is promised—eternal life.

God's Blueprint: *Putting God's Word into Your Relationship*

As you read the Bible's words aloud, notice how we are told to view trials.

HEBREWS 10:36
YOU NEED TO PERSEVERE SO THAT WHEN
YOU HAVE DONE THE WILL OF GOD, YOU WILL
RECEIVE WHAT HE HAS PROMISED.

JAMES 1:2–4
CONSIDER IT PURE JOY, MY BROTHERS AND SISTERS,
WHENEVER YOU FACE TRIALS OF MANY KINDS,
BECAUSE YOU KNOW THAT THE TESTING OF YOUR
FAITH PRODUCES PERSEVERANCE. LET PERSEVERANCE
FINISH ITS WORK SO THAT YOU MAY BE MATURE
AND COMPLETE, NOT LACKING ANYTHING.

As you work through the questions below, pay close attention to what your loved one is saying about what has been difficult in his or her life.

1. How does Mia's life and trials give you hope?
2. Have you ever had to persevere through a trial you thought would take you under? How did you fare? Has the experience strengthened or weakened you?
3. How do you think God uses trials to grow and mature us?
4. Share with your mate how he or she has helped you persevere through a trial.

Home Improvement: *Start Where You Are and Grow*

1. What can you learn as a couple from Mia's story that will help you raise your children to be mouthpieces for God?
2. What things can you do to have the right attitude about facing trials and difficulties?
3. How can you help your mate persevere under life's trials to gain a heavenly reward?

Write about what you can do for yourself and for your mate that will help you endure hard times.

HER THOUGHTS

_____

_____

_____

_____

_____

_____

_____

_____

_____

His Thoughts

_____

_____

_____

_____

_____

_____

_____

_____

_____

Team Building: *Grow Closer to Each Other as You Talk to God Together*

Read our prayers together and out loud, then pray together about how you can persevere through your own trials and how to turn your trials into His story.

AL: Father, I am grateful for all my nephews and nieces as they are such a blessing to my spirit. The strength and perseverance of Mia inspires me to stay strong through difficult days. I thank You for her and for Jase and Missy's endurance, and pray for blessings on their lives as she grows into a young woman. I also pray You will help me to show grit and determination through my own trials and to use every difficulty to bless someone else's life with hope. I am so thankful for all that You have brought me through, especially for the salvation I have in Christ. Through Him I pray, amen.

LISA: Heavenly Father, thank You for Mia. She is a blessing to our family. Thank You for giving Jase and Missy the strength to endure the trials and to persevere even when it was heartbreaking to do so. Please God, keep Mia safe in Your arms and allow her the opportunity to tell her story, which is really Your story. In Him I pray, amen.

The Power of Change

EARLY IN OUR relationship we each believed that we had the power to change the other into what we thought he or she needed to be. We have seen this common mistake repeated again and again in so many couples we have counseled. *If only you could fix him* or *if only you could make her do this or that* is the thinking process that leads to much relationship frustration. We've felt this frustration ourselves and been asked over and over by many couples to fix him or her. The simple truth is that change is powerful and doable, but only when a person makes the choice to change because he or she wants to or has to. When we began to practice and live this truth, our relationship began to soar.

One of the greatest biblical examples of this truth is the life of Jacob. We encourage you to read about him in Genesis 27–33. His name meant *deceiver,* and that is exactly what he was guilty of as he conspired with his mom to steal the birthright and blessing of his older twin brother, Esau, who hated him so much he wanted to kill him. Jacob was later duped by his future father-in-law and wound up marrying four women and having twelve sons, creating a blended-family nightmare, rife with constant jealousy, intrigue, and disharmony. Jacob wrestled with God one night and came to the realization that he needed to submit and change. The next day God changed his name to Israel, and Jacob became a better man and humbly asked forgiveness from his brother, which was given.

A lot of people will tell you they can't or won't change, and therefore, they stay stuck. But God tells us that the impossible is made possible through His power. We have experienced the blessing of change, but only when we humbled ourselves before God and requested His help.

We encourage you to look at the areas in your life that you previously thought were impossible to change and give God the opportunity to show you what He is capable of doing.

God's Blueprint: *Putting God's Word into Your Relationship*

As you read the verse below out loud, consider how your becoming like a child would help you make needed changes.

MATTHEW 18:2–4

HE CALLED A LITTLE CHILD TO HIM, AND PLACED THE
CHILD AMONG THEM. AND HE SAID: "TRULY I TELL YOU,
UNLESS YOU CHANGE AND BECOME LIKE LITTLE CHILDREN,
YOU WILL NEVER ENTER THE KINGDOM OF HEAVEN.
THEREFORE, WHOEVER TAKES THE LOWLY POSITION OF THIS
CHILD IS THE GREATEST IN THE KINGDOM OF HEAVEN.

As you discuss the questions below, remember to think more about changing yourself than about changing your loved one.

1. What does Jesus tell people to do in this text? What would this change look like?
2. What are some positive things you have changed about yourself since your relationship began?
3. What are some positive changes your mate has made that have impacted you?
4. Have you ever tried to change something about each other? How did it work out?

Home Improvement: *Start Where You Are and Grow*

1. What are some things your mate would like you to change about yourself?
2. What are some things you would like to change about yourself?
3. What are some things you need to be doing to better assess what might need to be changed?

Take time to look honestly into your heart and write about what you know God wants you to change in yourself.

HER THOUGHTS

_____

_____

_____

_____

_____

_____

_____

_____

_____

His Thoughts

_____

_____

_____

_____

_____

_____

_____

_____

_____

Team Building: *Grow Closer to Each Other as You Talk to God Together*

Read our prayers together and out loud, then pray together about having the courage to make the changes needed in your lives.

AL: Father, You have changed so many things in me through the years, and I am eternally grateful for all You've done for me. I know there are still things I need to work on and that change will always be a huge part of my spiritual growth. Help me to never be so prideful that I don't listen to the voice of reason whenever a change is needed in my life. Thank You for helping my beloved see the need for her own changes. Bless us as we strive to be more like You and to understand Your good, pleasing, and perfect will for our lives. In Jesus' name we pray, amen.

LISA: Father, I am a sinful human, and I need Your forgiveness. I need Your strength and power to change the areas of my life that do not reflect You and Your goodness. You have made me a different person already, but I want to be like You in every way. Continue to work your magic in me to change the things that make me a sinful person. Thank You for the changes You've already made in my marriage and my mate. Together, the three of us can overcome anything. In Your Son's name I pray, amen.

TAKING A STAND

W HEN MISS KAY talks about her early relationship woes with Phil, she always refers to the advice given to her by her grandmother when she was a young girl. She never forgot what Nannie told her one day: she told her granddaughter that one day she would have to fight for her marriage. Nannie proved to be prophetic! Miss Kay had every reason to run away from a difficult, unfaithful husband, but she decided to do all she could to fight for her family's survival. Ultimately, Phil came around and allowed God to change and remake him, and has been rewarded with a life of love and triumph. If you have been blessed in any way by our family or our television show, aren't you glad she fought for her marriage?

Human nature makes any of us want to run when faced with hard choices. Jonah is a famous runner in the Bible. He ran when he received a word from God he didn't want to hear. We encourage you to read that short book in the Bible because it is a whale of a tale! We aren't sure whether Jonah ever really changed his heart about his assignment, but when he finally did what God asked him to, other people's lives were changed, in spite of his own lackluster attitude.

Every one of us will face some evil in our own lives or in our relationships, and how we stand will make the difference in whether we triumph or fail. In Ephesians 6:10–20, Paul describes what kind of armor we need to be wearing when evil visits us. Take some time to read that passage and discuss what might be missing from your armor.

We encourage you to fight for your marriage and for your family and to never back down from the power of evil and destruction.

God's Blueprint: *Putting God's Word into Your Relationship*

As you read this scripture out loud, notice what you are to do both before and after "you have done everything."

EPHESIANS 6:13

THEREFORE PUT ON THE FULL ARMOR OF GOD, SO
THAT WHEN THE DAY OF EVIL COMES, YOU MAY
BE ABLE TO STAND YOUR GROUND, AND AFTER
YOU HAVE DONE EVERYTHING, TO STAND.

As you go through the questions below, be honest with each other about your strengths as well as your weaknesses.

1. Why can't we outrun our problems? What did you learn from reading about Jonah?
2. What "days of evil" have you already faced in your family?
3. Which parts of your armor are your strengths? Where are your weaknesses?
4. Tell your loved one what piece of armor that he or she wears has blessed you the most.

Home Improvement: *Start Where You Are and Grow*

1. What can you as a couple do to prepare yourselves better for attacks on your relationship and your family?
2. What weapons do you need to add to your spiritual arsenal to fight against evil?

Go back and reread Ephesians 6:10–20 and let that passage guide your writing today.

HER THOUGHTS

_____

_____

_____

_____

_____

_____

_____

_____

_____

HIS THOUGHTS

_____

_____

_____

_____

_____

_____

_____

_____

_____

Team Building: *Grow Closer to Each Other as You Talk to God Together*

Read our prayers together and out loud, then pray together about adding to your suit of armor.

AL: Father, we are so grateful You give us such great weapons to fight against evil. The weapon of prayer is one of the most important; I am honored to be able to tell You anything and know that You are listening and helping me. I thank You that Your Holy Spirit is active with my own spirit, and I humbly ask for less of me and more of Him in my everyday life. I pray for the wisdom to rightly handle the armor You have given me, and I ask for guidance as I lead my family and stand ready for attack. Thank You for Jesus and His protection. It's through Him that I stand and pray, amen.

LISA: God, so many times I have wanted to run like Jonah. Many times, I have not liked the task You have put before me. Other times, I don't like the people You put before me. Humble me, Father, to embrace each task and each person You want me to encounter and to shine Your light on each and every person and situation You bring my way. Help me to bring my requests before You more often. Help me to use the power of prayer and be the woman You created me to be. Because of Jesus I pray, amen.

DOLLARS AND SENSE

ONE OF THE most difficult issues most couples deal with is money. There never seems to be enough, and deciding how to spend what you do have leads to a lot of conflict. Like most couples, we have not been immune to money issues and have struggled with those issues in different ways throughout our marriage. The past few years we have finally found peace in this area of our lives thanks to a couple of realizations. First of all, we realized that we needed to be better stewards and managers of what we do have; secondly and more important, we finally decided that no possession on this earth is more important than the eternal home that awaits us in heaven.

Jesus' consistent message about money and possessions was, Don't get consumed with riches, building wealth, or what you leave here on earth. In Luke 12, He talked about a man who built bigger and bigger barns to hold his wealth, only to die with no plan for what lies beyond this life. In Luke 16, He talked about a man who had money and power on earth but refused to help a man who had neither. After their deaths, the rich man had a rude awakening to what a huge mistake he had made. In Luke 18, Jesus challenged a rich young ruler to give away his earthly wealth and follow Him, only to have this man walk sadly away because he loved his possessions more. You get the idea. Earthly wealth is just not worth fighting for or fighting about!

A family has to work, eat, manage, and navigate this life, but every one of us will leave this earth exactly as we came into it—with no possessions! Someone once said that you never see a hearse pulling a U-Haul trailer, and that is so true.

We encourage you to strive to store up your treasure in heaven and know that no possession on this earth is worth dying for.

God's Blueprint: *Putting God's Word into Your Relationship*

As you read the scriptures below, think about what kind of guards you need to put up in your life to protect your relationship against greed.

LUKE 12:15

THEN HE SAID TO THEM, "WATCH OUT! BE ON YOUR GUARD AGAINST ALL KINDS OF GREED; LIFE DOES NOT CONSIST IN AN ABUNDANCE OF POSSESSIONS."

LUKE 16:13

"NO ONE CAN SERVE TWO MASTERS. EITHER YOU WILL HATE THE ONE AND LOVE THE OTHER, OR YOU WILL BE DEVOTED TO THE ONE AND DESPISE THE OTHER. YOU CANNOT SERVE BOTH GOD AND MONEY."

Consider the following questions not only as individuals but especially as a couple.

1. What issues have you had pertaining to money or possessions?
2. Do you think there is truth in the notion that if you had enough money, you would have fewer problems? Is that a godly notion?
3. How should you deal with your money and possessions according to Jesus?
4. Tell your mate about a time he or she made you proud in the way he or she handled money.

Home Improvement: *Start Where You Are and Grow*

1. What do you need to change about how you view your collective money and possessions?
2. As a couple, how can you wisely provide for your family without being consumed by your money and future here on earth?
3. What are some things you need to begin doing to make sure you are storing treasure in heaven, not here on earth?

You might use this time to write out a plan for how to manage and steward your money in the future.

HER THOUGHTS

_____

_____

_____

_____

_____

_____

_____

_____

His Thoughts

_____

_____

_____

_____

_____

_____

_____

_____

_____

Team Building: *Grow Closer to Each Other as You Talk to God Together*

Read our prayers together and out loud, then pray together about stewarding your money well.

AL: Father, I came into this world a naked baby without a cent to my name, and I know I will leave it the same way. Help me not to fret over what I have or don't have, and help us to use the things we do have to store treasure in heaven, where it really matters. Forgive me when I forget this important lesson. Thank You for Jesus, my co-heir for the entire universe. In Him I pray, amen.

LISA: Lord, You have blessed me so richly in every area of my life. I have not always been the good steward I needed to be, but I do not sit and worry about whether You will provide for me. I know you will. Help me to be mindful of our money and know that it is from You and that I need to use it to advance Your kingdom. You give it, and You can take it away. Help me be content with whatever You give us. In Jesus' name, amen.

MEETING OUR NEEDS

WE HAVE BEEN blessed throughout our marriage by many different books and experiences that have helped grow our relationship. One book that really helped us was Willard Harley's *His Needs, Her Needs*. Dr. Harley discovered a consistent pattern of needs he continued to see being unmet in the couples he counseled. He came up with ten basic needs for most couples that vary in importance based on individuals: affection, sexual fulfillment, conversation, recreational companionship, honesty and openness, an attractive spouse, financial support, domestic support, family commitment, and admiration. We encourage you to get this book and read and discuss it. It will be a blessing to your relationship.

We used to think it was selfish to talk about what we need, but we have realized over time that God made us with these needs and that the human nature He gave us causes these desires. We are made up of three basic parts, and each of those parts has needs. There is a physical part, an emotional part, and a spiritual part. All three of these must be attended to in order for us to survive and thrive here on earth. When someone begins a relationship with another person, these same three areas will have needs that must be met, and if they aren't, the relationship will break down and be unhealthy.

We have to openly discuss all three areas of our needs fairly frequently because we have discovered that our needs change as we change and our circumstances change. With every new season in our lives, we have to shuffle the deck and make sure we are meeting each other's needs.

We encourage you to talk about your physical, emotional, and spiritual needs with your mate and make sure you are both doing everything possible to make sure no need goes unmet.

God's Blueprint: *Putting God's Word into Your Relationship*

As you read the passage below, think about how your words fulfill or deny the needs of your mate.

EPHESIANS 4:29

DO NOT LET ANY UNWHOLESOME TALK COME OUT
OF YOUR MOUTHS, BUT ONLY WHAT IS HELPFUL FOR
BUILDING OTHERS UP ACCORDING TO THEIR NEEDS,
THAT IT MAY BENEFIT THOSE WHO LISTEN.

Use these questions to understand more about each other and how you can help meet each other's needs.

1. Out of the three areas that make up our person (physical, emotional, and spiritual), in which area do you have the most needs? Why do think that is?
2. How did your upbringing and background shape your needs?
3. How have your relationship needs changed over time?

Home Improvement: *Start Where You Are and Grow*

1. What would you identify as your top five relationship needs?
2. What would you identify as your mate's top five relationship needs?
3. What things can you do to better meet the needs of your mate?
4. Tell your loved one at least one way he or she meets your needs.

Now that you understand your own and your mate's needs better, you might write about meeting your mate's needs and also about how you can clearly and kindly communicate your needs to your mate.

HER THOUGHTS

_____

_____

_____

_____

_____

_____

_____

_____

_____

His Thoughts

_____

_____

_____

_____

_____

_____

_____

_____

_____

Team Building: *Grow Closer to Each Other as You Talk to God Together*

Read our prayers together and out loud, then pray together about being aware of and meeting each other's needs.

AL: Father, I thank You for creating me in Your image. I know that You are three parts and that I am too. I pray I will not be selfish, but open about the things I need from my mate to be healthy. I pray I will anticipate her needs and that neither of us will ever give the evil one an opportunity to tempt us because we are not taking care of each other. Forgive me when I fail You and Lisa, through Jesus I pray, amen.

LISA: Thank You, Father, for giving me the soul mate to help me get to heaven. We are grateful that You have made us aware of the needs we have. I pray I can always meet the spousal needs of my husband and that he will meet my needs as well. Keep Satan out of our marriage and make our marriage reflect Your glory. In Jesus' name, with the help of the Spirit, amen.

TRAINING YOUNGER WOMEN AND MEN

WE HAVE A great friend, Joneal Kirby, who has developed a ministry called Heartfelt. She goes around to churches and teaches the concept of older women mentoring younger women and teaching them the godly principles laid out in Titus 2. She launched this program several years ago at our church and the women (and men) have greatly benefited from it. We feel this ministry is really needed in our churches today because so many young families are not living around their parents and grandparents. When this group first began, Lisa was a "heart sister," and now that she has grown older and more mature, she is a "heart mom." Look up this ministry online at http://heartfeltministries.org. Our church also has a program called Authentic Manhood, that teaches and disciples younger men to be the men God intended them to be. In Titus 2, we see the responsibility God has placed on us to impact younger marriages and families. We work to answer the call to pay forward what God has done in our relationship.

These five verses have so much to say about what role we are to play in our churches. First, the older women must learn to be reverent—not slanderers, not addicted to spirits, but teachers of what is good. These older women are to teach these ways to the younger women and also teach them how to love their families. Older men are encouraged to live out an example of respectability, improved character, and integrity. We have taken these responsibilities to heart and worked to mentor young couples. When you are young and newly married, sometimes the ways of the world creep in, and if you don't have a mom or grandmother to help you with being a wife and mother, the world can bring severe difficulties into your relationship. That's why God, in His wisdom, gave us forever families. He provided older women and men whom we can respect and learn from. When we are learning to be self-controlled, pure, kind, and busy with our family, it leaves us less time to be discontent with our lives. We are also more respectful and loving toward each other.

We encourage you to get involved with the ministries of a growing, loving church so you can learn from and model what God is doing in others. Then, as you mature, you can pass on what God has done in you to others. Get involved and use the forever family God gave you to help you along life's journey.

God's Blueprint: *Putting God's Word into Your Relationship*

As you read the passage below, notice the specific characteristics it mentions.

TITUS 2:3–7

TEACH THE OLDER WOMEN TO BE REVERENT IN THE WAY THEY LIVE, NOT TO BE SLANDERERS OR ADDICTED TO MUCH WINE, BUT TO TEACH WHAT IS GOOD. THEN THEY CAN URGE THE YOUNGER WOMEN TO LOVE THEIR HUSBANDS AND CHILDREN, TO BE SELF-CONTROLLED AND PURE, TO BE BUSY AT HOME, TO BE KIND, AND TO BE SUBJECT TO THEIR HUSBANDS, SO THAT NO ONE WILL MALIGN THE WORD OF GOD. SIMILARLY, ENCOURAGE THE YOUNG MEN TO BE SELF-CONTROLLED. IN EVERYTHING SET THEM AN EXAMPLE BY DOING WHAT IS GOOD.

As you answer the questions below, think about how you can grow together as a couple.

1. Who is someone you look up to spiritually? Why?
2. Are you currently involved in any mentoring relationships or programs to strengthen your spiritual lives and/or relationship?
3. If you are not involved yet, where is a good place to start? If you are involved, what are some ways to improve?

Home Improvement: *Start Where You Are and Grow*

1. What, specifically, can you do as a couple to be a better example of what Christ wants all of us to be?
2. What specific things do we need to be praying about so we can help others learn what God wants for their marriages and lives?
3. Share with your spouse what he or she is already doing that is worth being passed on to others.

Write about what you, individually, want to pass on to others and what you want to pass on as a couple.

HER THOUGHTS

_____

_____

_____

_____

_____

_____

_____

_____

His Thoughts

_____

_____

_____

_____

_____

_____

_____

_____

_____

Team Building: *Grow Closer to Each Other as You Talk to God Together*

Read our prayers together and out loud, then pray together about how you can pass on what you know while you also follow the good example of others.

AL: Lord, I am so grateful for the men You have put in my life whose example I can emulate and follow regarding what a real man looks like. You have grown me in so many ways, but I still have so much to learn and so much more to do. Lead me to young men I can impact for Your glory and help me always look to men older than I who can show me how to be more like Christ. I pray this prayer through Jesus, my Mentor, amen.

LISA: Father, I am grateful for our Titus 2 ministry, and I am grateful You laid this on Joneal's heart to put into action. I pray I can teach other people and empower other women to begin a ministry that teaches others the power of being a mentor to younger women. Use me, Lord, to benefit other women. I am Your vessel to be used for Your Glory. In His name, amen.

CO-HEIRS IN CHRIST

WHEN YOU WERE growing up, what did you want your life to be like when you got married? Did you have a good example to look at in your parents', grandparents', or friends' marriage? In our own families, we saw the good, the bad, and the ugly, but ultimately, we saw marriages and families that worked toward the right goals. We have had the blessing of seeing a lot of marriages that were great examples. One of those examples is a couple we have worked with, gone to church with, and been mentored by named Carl and Barbara Allison. Carl went home to be with the Lord in December of 2013, but he was one of the greatest men we ever knew. Barbara adored Carl, and Carl thought Barbara hung the moon. She was submissive to him, and he respected and protected her. What a blessing to have examples like this to follow!

In 1 Peter 3:1–7, the example laid out for all marriages by the apostle Peter is one of submission and respect. Peter says that women are to be submissive to their husbands and that husbands are to respect and care for their wives. He also says that men and women are *co-heirs* with Christ. That means that they will both have the same eternal inheritance.

Peter says that the reason a woman should respect her husband is for the sake of his eternal destiny. If he is not a believer, then he will see her example and turn to the Lord. He goes on to say that submission produces purity and reverence. He says that beauty does not come from what women wear, how they fix their hair, or how they use their makeup. He says beauty comes from a gentle and quiet spirit. Lisa has always struggled with this passage because she doesn't see herself as a gentle and quiet person, but I remind her that Peter says that it's a "gentle and quiet *spirit*" that is of great value to God. Peter also says that hope in God is beautiful, and it's true that women who have hope for an eternal future tend to have a more beautiful outlook on life and family than women who have no hope at all.

Peter goes on to tell husbands that they must respect their wives and care for them. He says that not doing so could "hinder" their prayers. Husbands are to love and respect their wives as co-heirs with them in the gift of life. In Ephesians 5:21, the apostle Paul adds that men and women are to submit to one another as believers, just as Christ submitted Himself to the Father to provide eternal life for all of us.

We encourage you to look at this text and see that submission and respect are foundational to a healthy marriage. As we submit to Christ, let's submit to one another out of love and respect, and in view of eternal life.

God's Blueprint: *Putting God's Word into Your Relationship*

As you read the passage below, open your hearts to Peter's teaching—even if some of this is hard to accept.

1 PETER 3:1–4, 7

WIVES, IN THE SAME WAY SUBMIT YOURSELVES
TO YOUR OWN HUSBANDS SO THAT, IF ANY OF THEM
DO NOT BELIEVE THE WORD, THEY MAY BE WON OVER
WITHOUT WORDS BY THE BEHAVIOR OF THEIR WIVES,
WHEN THEY SEE THE PURITY AND REVERENCE OF
YOUR LIVES. YOUR BEAUTY SHOULD NOT COME
FROM OUTWARD ADORNMENT, SUCH AS ELABORATE
HAIRSTYLES AND THE WEARING OF GOLD JEWELRY
OR FINE CLOTHES. RATHER, IT SHOULD BE THAT
OF YOUR INNER SELF, THE UNFADING BEAUTY OF
A GENTLE AND QUIET SPIRIT, WHICH IS OF GREAT WORTH
IN GOD'S SIGHT. . . . HUSBANDS, IN THE SAME WAY
BE CONSIDERATE AS YOU LIVE WITH YOUR WIVES,
AND TREAT THEM WITH RESPECT AS THE WEAKER PARTNER
AND AS HEIRS WITH YOU OF THE GRACIOUS GIFT
OF LIFE, SO THAT NOTHING WILL HINDER YOUR PRAYERS.

Be open to what God is teaching you as you talk together.

1. What couple would you like to emulate in your marriage? What are they doing that seems to work well?

2. What is difficult about submitting yourself to another person?
3. Based on this passage in 1 Peter, how would you define beauty in each other?
4. Tell your spouse at least one thing you see in him or her that other couples can emulate.

Home Improvement: *Start Where You Are and Grow*

1. What can you do to be more respectful and submissive in your relationship with God?
2. What can you do to be more respectful or more submissive to your mate?

Write about how this week's passage made you feel and about new convictions you developed.

HER THOUGHTS

_____

_____

_____

_____

_____

_____

_____

_____

_____

_____

_____

_____

_____

_____

_____

_____

_____

_____

Team Building: *Grow Closer to Each Other as You Talk to God Together*

Read our prayers together and out loud, then pray together about what you learned this week.

AL: Lord, I thank You for the love, respect, and submission of Your Son, Jesus, and the other great examples You have put in our lives. I pray I will always treat my mate with the utmost care and respect and that we will be an example to others. Thank You for her and for Christ. Through Him, amen.

LISA: Father, I struggle with that "quiet and gentle spirit." I am learning through Your Scripture how to be more submissive and more respectful. Help me to see that my beauty is from You. You have placed a hope inside me that one day I will spend eternity with You. Teach me Your ways. Create a quiet and gentle spirit within me. In Jesus' name, amen.

VOWS ARE TO BE KEPT

HOW MANY VOWS have you made in your life? Most of us make at least one. Since you are reading a couples devotional, then you've probably made two. The first was to God to be His servant. The second was to your soul mate in front of an official and some witnesses. You get the idea that vows are sacred and meant to be kept and certainly shouldn't be made in haste. But these vows are sometimes hard to keep, right? That's why the preacher usually says, "For better or worse; in sickness or health; for richer or poorer." Keeping your vow through difficulty is sort of the idea behind making the vow to begin with!

In Judges 11, we read of a man named Jephthah who made a vow to God. He asked God to give him victory over his enemies and vowed that in exchange for the victory, he would sacrifice as a burnt offering whatever came out of his house upon his return. Who knows what he thought would come out of that house, but we're pretty sure he didn't expect it to be his only child. But it was. Amazingly, he kept his vow. Was this vow hasty and unwise? We think so, and we both agree we wouldn't make that vow, but we do give the man credit for staying true to the vow he made to God. We encourage you to read that sad chapter and think about how God views vows.

When we had our most devastating marriage problems fifteen

years ago, Al made a vow to me and to God. He chose to forgive me for being unfaithful, and he vowed to never use that sin to hurt us or our marriage. He vowed he would use our past only to help others. A few months into this vow, I was dishonest with him again, and he knew it. But he had made a vow to God. He waited for me to confess the sin, and then he once again forgave my dishonesty. Was it easy for him to do that? No! But he made a vow, and a vow is to be kept through hurts, dishonesty, fear, and resentment. I am so thankful he kept his vow.

We implore you to keep your vows to God and each other. If there is a time when you need to make an additional vow, think about it carefully. Don't make it in haste. A vow is meant to be kept.

God's Blueprint: *Putting God's Word into Your Relationship*

As you read this scripture out loud, notice several things the passage below says about vows.

ECCLESIASTES 5:4–6

WHEN YOU MAKE A VOW TO GOD, DO NOT DELAY TO FULFILL IT. HE HAS NO PLEASURE IN FOOLS; FULFILL YOUR VOW. IT IS BETTER NOT TO MAKE A VOW THAN TO MAKE ONE AND NOT FULFILL IT. DO NOT LET YOUR MOUTH LEAD YOU INTO SIN.

As you talk about the questions below, think seriously about the vows you've made to each other and to others.

1. What are your thoughts on the vow Jephthah made with God?
2. Why is it a good idea to limit your vows to really important decisions? Why do you think Al made the vow to Lisa and to God about forgiveness?
3. Have you ever made a vow you didn't keep? What effect did it have on you?
4. Share with your mate a time when he or she kept a promise to you and how that made you feel.

Home Improvement: *Start Where You Are and Grow*

1. What vows have you made to God? What vows have you made to your mate? What vows have you made to others?
2. What changes do you need to make so that you will *start* holding to or hold *better* to your vows?
3. What can you do to help your mate better hold to his or her vows made to God or you?

Write about what you learned about vows this week and how this will impact your personal life and your marriage.

HER THOUGHTS

_____

_____

_____

_____

_____

_____

_____

_____

_____

HIS THOUGHTS

_____

_____

_____

_____

_____

_____

_____

_____

_____

Team Building: *Grow Closer to Each Other as You Talk to God Together*

Read our prayers together and out loud, then pray together about being careful in choosing what vows you make and committed in keeping those you do make.

AL: Lord, the vow I made to be Your servant is still the most important decision I ever made. I am as committed to You today as when I was a teenager. I pray for Your guidance and wisdom as I continue to navigate the river that is my life. I also continue to hold to my vow to my beloved and my commitment to never harm her or us. Thank You for showing me the possibilities of grace and the pathway to healing in our marriage. We give You all the glory through the presence of Your Son and with the help of Your Spirit. Amen.

LISA: Father God, I take my vows seriously. I know You take them seriously too. Help me each day to be conscientious of the vows I've made to You and the vows I made to Al. I pray that each time I think of our vows, I will also think of the reasons I made them. Through Your Son, our Savior, I pray, amen.

WEEK 52

THE MAIN THING

T HE MOST IMPORTANT thing any couple can learn is the one thing that motivates us above all else. What is the one thing we build everything else off of? What is our foundation for living, loving, and building our lives and our legacy? Our hope and our prayer is that your answer is the same as ours. The gospel story of Jesus Christ is our motivation to live, and we have dedicated every ounce of who we are and what we have to making sure we are counted among the believers when Jesus returns to this planet the same way He left.

We have struggled throughout our years together, but the more we put our earthly selves to death, the more our spiritual selves have come to life. Not coincidentally, our relationship has soared and strengthened as our lives have changed for the better. We have been open about our sinfulness and our shortcomings because we want other people to know that anyone can be saved, no matter what they have done. We will be unashamed when the Lord returns because He took our sin, our shame, and our weaknesses and triumphantly nailed them to an executioner's cross over two thousand years ago.

We implore you to give yourself to Christ, if you haven't already, then be prepared to grow in ways you never thought possible. As a forgiven son or daughter, you will finally have the tools to build a powerful relationship—even through trials and difficult times.

We challenge you to dedicate yourself to learning and living by the Bible and to be prepared to have a family that functions amazingly well, in spite of all the typical challenges. We pray a blessing upon your relationship and look forward to meeting you one day in eternity.

God's Blueprint: *Putting God's Word into Your Relationship*

As you read this scripture together, notice all the different things this passage says about the gospel.

1 CORINTHIANS 15:1–4

NOW, BROTHERS AND SISTERS, I WANT TO REMIND YOU OF THE GOSPEL I PREACHED TO YOU, WHICH YOU RECEIVED AND ON WHICH YOU HAVE TAKEN YOUR STAND. BY THIS GOSPEL YOU ARE SAVED, IF YOU HOLD FIRMLY TO THE WORD I PREACHED TO YOU. OTHERWISE, YOU HAVE BELIEVED IN VAIN. FOR WHAT I RECEIVED I PASSED ON TO YOU AS OF FIRST IMPORTANCE: THAT CHRIST DIED FOR OUR SINS ACCORDING TO THE SCRIPTURES, THAT HE WAS BURIED, THAT HE WAS RAISED ON THE THIRD DAY ACCORDING TO THE SCRIPTURES.

Be honest with each other about the questions below, even if it's a bit uncomfortable.

1. How would you describe where you are right now spiritually?
2. How does your heavenly ambition affect your earthly reality?
3. How will your family be blessed by your giving yourselves fully to Christ's care and control?

Home Improvement: *Start Where You Are and Grow*

1. What do you need to do to improve your spiritual standing?
2. What do you need to do to help your mate's spiritual standing?
3. What do you as a couple need to implement in order to increase your commitment to the gospel and the furthering of the kingdom of God?

As you write this week, carefully consider your beliefs about the gospel. Your eternity is at stake.

HER THOUGHTS

_____
_____
_____
_____
_____
_____
_____
_____
_____

HIS THOUGHTS

_____

_____

_____

_____

_____

_____

_____

_____

_____

Team Building: *Grow Closer to Each Other as You Talk to God Together*

Read our prayers together and out loud, then pray together about your commitment to the gospel of Christ.

AL: Lord, I can't properly express the joy I feel in knowing that I will spend eternity with You and with those I love the most here on earth. I await Your Son's coming with eager anticipation and want to take advantage of every opportunity here on earth to help others know what is waiting for those who believe and obey You. I thank you for my wife and the joy we share together in our commitment to You. Thank You for Your Holy Spirit who indwells me and Your Son who inspires me. With Their help I pray this prayer, amen.

LISA: Dear God, I am humbled by Your love for us. The plan of salvation You have for us is overwhelming. Just to think that You love us that much! Please, Father, send Your angels to protect us until Your coming, but come quickly. We can't wait to dwell in the house of our Lord forever! Because of Jesus' sacrifice I pray, amen.